KEEP THIS QUIET

KEEP THIS QUIET

My Relationship with Hunter S. Thompson, Milton Klonsky, and Jan Mensaert

Margaret A. Harrell

Saeculum University Press
USA Romania

To order in quantity at a discount, email orders@hunterthompsonnewbook.com

A particular thanks to Hunter Thompson Literary Executor Douglas Brinkley, Professor of History at Rice University, for permission to reprint from the Hunter S. Thompson letters and other materials

Book Interior design by Bram Larrick of wakingworld.com

Publisher's Cataloging-in-Publication Data

Harrell, Margaret A. (Margaret Ann).
Keep this quiet : my relationship with Hunter S. Thompson, Milton Klonsky, and Jan Mensaert / Margaret A. Harrell.
    p. cm.
    "Volume 1"
Includes bibliographical references and index.
ISBN 978-0-9837045-0-8 (pbk.)
ISBN 978-0-9837045-1-5 (e-book)
1. Thompson, Hunter S.—Correspondence. 2. Journalists—United States—Biography. 3. Greenwich Village (New York, N. Y.)—Biography. 4. Thompson, Hunter S.—Friends and associates. 5. Harrell, Margaret A.—Friends and associates. I. Title.

E169.12.H37 2011
306/.1097309046—dc22

                                                                    2011909464

Saeculum University Press
5048 Amber Clay Lane, Raleigh, NC 27612

A division of Saeculum U. P. S.
B-dul Victoriei 5-7; 550024 Sibiu, Romania

Advance Reader Comments

I gulped it—**Puiana Harvey**, C. G. Jung Institute Santa Fe

Entertaining and informative . . . This is a pleasure to read. I love the tone, which is a real achievement—even if it just came naturally—**George Stade**, author of *Equipment for Living: Literature, Moderns, Monsters, Popsters, and Us*

Like a radio station with its own incomparable frequency, the inspiring book tunes readers' receivers, sagaciously transporting them to . . . that quiet part of our psyche that knows no limitations or boundaries. Readers will experience new insights into the personal lives, talents, and the author's intimate relationships with Hunter S. Thompson, the father of Gonzo journalism and author of *Hell's Angels*; Milton Klonsky, New York City poet and Greenwich Village cult figure with transformative word power and magnetic personality; Jan Mensaert, Belgian poet combining concepts of his music with his poetry—the man the author married. Readers will be privy to never-before-published letters from Hunter Thompson, deepening insight into the turning point in his career and emergence into gonzo—**Bernie Nelson**, *The Mindquest Review*

Margaret Harrell from early on had as her goal to live the most meaningful life possible. Three mentor/lovers helped in turn to light her way: Hunter Thompson for his ability to see the world for himself through as few distorting cultural lens as possible; Milton Klonsky for his deep wisdom and nurturing of the intelligence and sensitivity he saw within her; and the man she married, the Belgium poet Jan Mensaert, who sought out extreme experiences, encouraging her to come along and test her own limits—**Virginia Parrott Williams**, coauthor of *Anger Kills* and *In Control*; President, Williams LifeSkills

Beautiful in its directness and its openness—**Chris Van de Velde,** Numenon Counseling Institute Director, Ghent, Belgium

Fascinating and riveting. *So there's a sequel? In progress?* What a story!!—**Mary Paul Thomas**, Raleigh, NC

To Hunter, for energizing this book in obvious and unobvious ways

You can tell a lot about a person from whether he eats green or black olives.

Hunter, first meeting, 1967

Acknowledgments

Correspondence from Hunter is reproduced by permission of Hunter Thompson Literary Executor Douglas Brinkley, Professor of History at Rice University. I gratefully acknowledge his support and his generosity with Thompson materials.

Permission to reprint a letter forty-four years old was kindly granted by Paul Krassner.

Permission to reveal David Pierce's secret role in *Hell's Angels* was kindly granted by Pierce.

Incalculable thanks to Virginia Parrott Williams, who tirelessly urged me to write in a "fact-fat" way, adding invaluable sharpness of insight and confidence in the book. A particular thanks to Jim Silberman for making possible my experience at Random House by his assignments, including Hunter's first book, and his current insights. Many thanks to critical expertise from Noel Baucom. To William Kennedy for anecdotes—and for putting me in touch with Rosalie Sorrels, who contributed stories and located Pierce. To William McKeen for encouragement. To the design team, Gaelyn Larrick for the cover, and Bram Larrick, for the interior, who knew just what the book needed. To my publisher, Didi-Ionel Cenuser. To Stacey Cochran, who edited the manuscript astutely. To Algonquin Executive Editor, Chuck Adams, for behind-the-scenes support. Finally, to all who played a role. And to Snoep, Snoepie, and Hans, my dachshunds—who watched me write.

Photography Credits

Hunter S. Thompson: front cover self-portrait, courtesy of his Estate

Robert John: Milton Klonsky

Jameson Weston (Hogle Zoo, Salt Lake City): Eastern Indigo Snake

Dan Beards: Random House (old Villard House)
TrueBlood Studio, Greenville, NC: Margaret (child)
Jan Mensaert: slides (Morocco and Belgium), courtesy of Het Toreke museum/archives
Unknown: Margaret (New York)

Drawing/Design Credits
Jan Mensaert: courtesy of Het Toreke (scanned by Harrie Spelmans)

Music Lyric Credits

SHE HAS FUNNY CARS
Words and Music by MARTY BALIN and JORMA KAUKONEN
Copyright © 1967 (Renewed) ICEBAG CORP.
All Rights Reserved   Used by Permission

TODAY
Words and Music by MARTY BALIN and JORMA KAUKONEN
Copyright © 1967 (Renewed) ICEBAG CORP.
All Rights Reserved   Used by Permission

COMIN' BACK TO ME
Words and Music by MARTY BALIN
Copyright © 1967 (Renewed) ICEBAG CORP.
All Rights Reserved   Used by Permission

AND I LIKE IT
Words and Music by MARTY BALIN and JORMA KAUKONEN
Copyright © 1967 (Renewed) ICEBAG CORP.
All Rights Reserved   Used by Permission

Contents

Preface

How does the Zeitgeist, the spirit of the times, manifest in the world, if not through people? There are certain individuals who through their lives capture the Zeitgeist of their times—they are people who pass into history as legendary figures. But they are also flesh-and-blood men and women who have a different impact on the world than the many others who stand by. The three men portrayed in this book are such men, inexplicably and inexorably driven to express the existential questions of their time. The Zeitgeist of the '60s was emerging through them. The postmodern. The deconstruction of the social norms that had prevailed until then.

Milton had more of a grounding in conventional society, more self-preservation—in a lot of ways spiritually wise. The other two consumed their own lives, not holding back, going as far as they could. Most people live tamely and vicariously. They were isolated. They lived their lives as an experiment, that could be teeth-jarring to the onlooker, embedded in the social and cultural substrate being uncomfortably peeled away.

Jan in his use of drugs and alcohol was quite clearly prepared to deconstruct himself, to sacrifice his own psychic container in order to let this molten kind of creativity burst out of it. But he didn't strengthen his container; he weakened it. Hunter did it not with his psyche but with his body. Hunter's psyche was pretty damn intact. But he was willing to take risks with his body. He had a lucidity about the altered states he was putting himself into. He could witness, in order to write about it afterwards.

But how could these three men be part of the same story, if not through their taste in a woman? In universal philosophical terms, they could be three male graces of the postmodern era: the triptych of Goodness, Beauty, and Truth. Milton representing goodness: mind, ethics; Jan beauty: the introspective, the aesthete; Hunter Truth: "fucking bullshit," physically noncompromising.

So this is a story of how three extraordinary men embodied and expressed the Zeitgeist of the time—the blossoming of the postmodern era—not just in their work, but in their own most intimate relationship with their bodies and their lives. The story unfolding here is seen through the eyes of a woman they loved. She saw it close up, being intimate with them, providing a glimpse of how they related to an intimate other that they wanted something from. But it doesn't put her in the middle, because she doesn't want to be in the middle.

Two might be an accident, but three— In the meantime, it's not their impact on her that made Margaret who she is, because she was already as is, as you will meet her here too.

Helen Titchen Beeth
Brussels, Belgium

Author's Note

I asked myself why write about these three men together in a book—why was that so important to me? Why not just isolate out Hunter? Not many remember the other two. I just happened to get to know them well enough to know (and preserve in this two-part memoir) a bit of their genius, which otherwise for most people would have dropped back into the collective bucket of humanity unnoted.

I thought my job of recording important. Hunter is at the center and his unpublished letters to me, almost all of which, too, otherwise would have gone down the drain of the dregs of humanity (without a copy, without a trace).

Prologue: My Personal Myth

It was August 31, 1968. I was in my Random House office, a cubicle that though small gave privacy. I was a copy editor and had resigned.

The head copy editor had tried to dissuade me. She said very few people could wake up every day without a structure—a job. She couldn't. She didn't believe I could. I said I needed more time to write. She said I'd be back. When I asked for extra time to clean out my desk, she would not extend the deadline. My decision that night is what makes this book—and a record of part of Hunter S. Thompson's life—possible.

I had waited till the last minute. It was late. The night watchman kept guard at the front door of the old mansion in which Random House had its quarters in New York City. A janitor had long ago emptied trash cans and vacuumed. I looked at the pile of orange-gold paper, letters from Hunter. Though many concerned the creation of *Hell's Angels*, others were written in the two years subsequent. I did not think that a relationship, however much it also involved a book, was anyone else's business. There was no way to separate the business part out. After midnight, bleary-eyed, I picked up the letters and swept out. Leaving Random House for the last time.

As it developed, there was no carbon copy of most, handwritten or typed on both sides.

I never considered publishing them before. I needed permission. An impossible hurdle. But Hunter, as if he'd thought of that, told his Literary Executor, Doug Brinkley, about me. No matter how long ago the story took place, it was alive in his memory, alive in mine. And though in a book—not on a tree—I decided to carve our initials.

The period covered in the two volumes is the late '60s through 1986 because in looking back, I found that that time length, nineteen years, made a unit. It cycled around in my life. Some early readers asked me, *Why were you with these guys?* I thought: *You've read the manuscript and still don't know.* Besides the romance, it was the lure of genius. How it makes the excitement race through the veins—about anything: an idea, a kiss, the prospect of a kiss. Every little detail made me feel more alive. And I wanted to feel alive. Going beyond that: Could I learn what they had to teach me? Why were they so perfect to fall in love with if one had a life purpose like mine???

I open *The Gonzo Tapes: The Life and Work of Dr. Hunter S. Thompson.* And time spins backwards . . . 1967. The Summer of Love. "San Francisco (Be Sure To Wear Some Flowers in Your Hair)"; Height-Ashbury, the hippy counterculture. *But what I remember is personal: meeting Hunter Thompson.* The other two males in this book, I've written about in the past but not Hunter. Never Hunter. I write this book, triggered by his death.

With *Jefferson Airplane Takes Off* blaring from the computer I remember. After six months of parrying back and forth with my telephone voice two/three time zones apart, in February Hunter was led into my Random House office; there I'd copy edited *Hell's Angels.* Preserved in a two-page spread in the booklet of *The Gonzo Tapes* is a picture of a couple of those orange-gold pages—with marks in two styles: his in black and red ink, mine in pencil. There, for a few moments in a cubbyhole just for me time stands still, is enscrawled like a signature. Memory halts. I walk in.

In a chapter up ahead, I go into the intensity of that meeting. Here I want to preview one scene. In freezing weather during his press tour we escaped to a Madison Avenue record shop. The Airplane's "Surrealistic Pillow" had just been released—the San Francisco sound. The line extended into the street. A salesperson hustled the crowd into a little room, then again into the cold. I was wearing low-heel pumps, the back open. In his Editor's Note to *Gonzo Letters* 2, Douglas Brinkley recounts how Hunter kept sampling, lifting the needle: "You can do whatever you please. The world's waiting to be seized." At the fourth track, "Today" ("To be any more than all I am would be a lie. . . . With you standing near I can tell the world what it means to love"), he broke into his big grin and said, "Today *is* my time." Indeed. And he knew it.

But my own private memory bank looks elsewhere: to "And I Like It" in the *first* album: "This is *my* life . . . my way . . . *my* time . . . Ain't gonna be like the rest." Our theme song. The lyrics warned not to "try to keep [him] tied." No, it was a given from the outset. And one more thing: he might need to "git away from the mess."

I'd been a writer since I could read. But never in the forty years since meeting Hunter did I publish but a single paragraph about him. He dedicated the Penguin *Hell's Angels* to me. It dropped out in proofing! The whole story slipped out of time, out of history.

If my life was to make sense, I could not get away forever with leaving him out of my biography. It had a missing facet, *all he represented deprived of its weight.* Over the years I sent him my books published in Romania—that brought into light other relationships. I wondered if he knew he was not omitted for reasons of memory. It would have taken a steely understanding and perspicacious sense of "reality," which he had. It seemed a pact to speak not one word about him in print. But then, who was the pact with? In the late '80s I had this dream that died in a matter of months, evidently incinerated in midair—about helping write "The Hunter Thompson Story." There was no time frame. It was vivid, a certainty. But nothing happened. So I had the instruction. From whom, I didn't know. But I was sure it was some sort of fact, somewhere. These intense dream communications don't always amount to anything in fact, though often they do. They are, in any case, information.

Over time I dreaded hearing a TV announcer say he was dead. Then a few weeks before February 20, '05, waking from a forgotten dream, I felt an excited closeness to Hunter, that mysteriously everything was fine. A few weeks later hearing CNN announce his suicide, I watched my feelings. Not crushed. I felt the dream atmosphere rise up, that it was all right, everything was all right, and I began to hear in my head: "Please don't let me be misunderstood." It was about at that moment I acquired the sharp intention to write this book. My idea was to remain a dim figure in the background. But I found I had to step forward. Acquire some flesh and blood.

I had not one, not two—but three—ways to sample a particular philosophy, in men in the mid–late 1960s in New York City: they were audacious standouts, originals, flamboyant to different degrees, flamingly, defiantly nonconformist.

To me, it seemed the extraordinary was the path into life. The basic philosophy was there: "Don't sleep through your life. Dare and dare again. LIVE. It doesn't matter if you die young, even. Give back to life the energy it gave you potentially. Sense potential. Don't wait to see it standing there in front of you *in someone else*. Make memories. Make joy. Fill your basket with dreams, moments of being fully alive—*not knowing what would happen the next instant*. Quick, it's fleeting past. No, you caught it. Catch it while it's undecided, difficult, no guarantees, no conditions."

"Carcassonne," by William Faulkner, is one of his most famous statements on creativity: *And me on a buckskin pony with eyes like blue electricity and a mane like tangled fire, galloping up the hill and right off into the high heaven of the world.*[1] Now compare this to Hunter Thompson on death:

> my concept of death for a long time was to come down that mountain road at a hundred twenty and just keep going straight right there, burst out through the barrier and hang out above all that . . . and there I'd be, sitting in the front seat, stark naked, with a case of whiskey next to me, and a case of dynamite in the trunk, or *boot*, it would be in a Jaguar, honking the horn, and the lights on, and just sit there in space for an instant, a human bomb, and then fall on down into that mess of steel mills. It'd be a tremendous goddamn explosion. No pain. No one would get hurt. I'm pretty sure,

unless they've changed the highway, that launching place is still there. As soon as I get home, I ought to take the drive and just check it out.[2]

But who goes over the edge? Where is the snow leopard Hunter liked? that "high white sound"? In the experience of liberated, unfettered creativity experienced *by anyone who lets go the reins of conformity* and discovers what spark drives the heart within, be it St. Teresa getting pins stuck in her by the Church or any other form against the mold. So I want to look at Hunter this way, not through rules he broke as a bad boy. But with the soaring spirit in each of us that drives self-expression, all too often tamped down unlike in the descriptions here. Everyone can loose their inner fire. The cost is lack of security facing the Unknown. The possible reward is Self-Illumination, pure Joy. Like Faulkner, Hunter wanted to leave his life in stone tablets, mark time with a sign KILROY WAS HERE. As the Airplane said, "Small things like reasons are put into a jar."

At twenty-six I would race over to Carnegie Hall at lunchtime. From Fiftieth and Madison was fifteen minutes. There I'd take the only class available, ballet for children ten to eleven. I was two heads taller, doing precision *jetés* or *battement tendus* across the floor. I loved to gracefully extend my leg, turning my head precisely with or opposite it. So here I am, forty years later, racing to a class—the closest, just five minutes. In one of my ballet classes it's me and the ten-to-fifteen-year-olds; in another, thirteen to adult. In modern dance thirteen to adult. But that's what keeps me out of traffic. No, I do not look ridiculous. They can pirouette and leap, but astonishingly, most of the time I keep up. Besides, they are outrageously nice to me.

I am rushing off to class. Everyone I teach personal growth to can easily imagine me there. But it would be a giant jump to put together the me who teaches "light body" and the one who copy edited Hunter S. Thompson. What connected them? I teach in the *now*. This is who I am. Sometimes a few flashbacks to the spiritual initiations. But almost never a story from *then*, the wild days, as it were. Only, I didn't consider myself wild. I didn't even know that I had a flamboyant side, and until my roommate told me at forty-three, "I would never let a boyfriend of mine near you," I didn't suspect I made a femme fatale impression on some people. But I'm glad to have my hidden stash of memories that no hard times can take away.

I ponder what it all means. And I see the child: me, two years old. That child, that moment when I decided who I would be. Just two, and the question already came up, *Margaret, what kind of life will you have? Will it be a Prufrock measuring out your life in coffee spoons, not daring to walk in water with your trousers rolled? Or on the edge, not knowing what comes next? Not knowing where a decision will lead?* I didn't know I decided it then and there, in a simple impulse. But Carl Jung says that we all have a personal myth. Everyone. No longer are myths primarily found in collective stories that the whole tribe believes.

PART ONE

The Top of the Stairs

My first memory is of myself at the top of the stairs, wondering whether to go down. I was about two years old. I had somehow gotten out of bed. That, I don't remember. Nor do I remember noticing the banister that I would grow up to slide down or the pastel oranges of the trees outside—just the sense of weighing a question. My father had a poker game going on. What interested me was joining them in the living room. This great internal battle raged for some minutes.

I tiptoed in. The men were smoking cigars. Next thing I knew my uncle Hunter lifted me into his lap. My dazzled eyes beheld rims of bright cards one behind the other. Then he fanned out his hand close to my face. As his tight-curled fingers opened wide just for me I felt let in on a secret—betting, a game under way . . . A sense of things hidden under the surface: there, the real story was played in concealed hands.

It was World War II when this battle between me and me took place, whether to listen to myself and descend into the skirmish or remain in my perch. Anyway, that was my first memory, an intuition, an instinct, a natural expression of me before I learned too much how to act in the world.

The three male relationships in this book set the foundation for the next part of my life, which—though it looks very different— needed that to build on. I had this tremendous drive. Yet only half of me was fearless, the introverted half. Who could pull the fear out of me? Who could show me the mirror of my fearlessness deep within?

The small town of Greenville had no theater. But every year Uncle Hunter, who was not my real uncle, did Vaudeville-like skits with song and dance in a Kiwanis Minstrel barbershop quartet to raise money for charity. The soul music gyrated in the room. In-jolting a spirit of life to me. Only incidentally did I notice the blacked-up faces. "Pack Up Your Troubles in Your Old Kit Bag" was, to me, like (later) Gene Kelly in *Singin' in the Rain*—as if my uncle Hunter was projecting a theme song to me from the stage. I watched, drank in the banjos, and thought: *Anything is possible.*

Behind our two-story red-brick house was a large woods crossed by railroad tracks and a trestle bridge that I was scared to walk across but frequently did, as a short cut to school. The air smelled of honey-suckle. Living just inside the city limits, we played in vacant lots with haystacks and wild strawberries. But what I loved was the lot next door, where thin white vines hung from tree branches; we sometimes swung on them as in *Tarzan*. In the little woods copperheads, rattle-snakes, cottonmouths, and garden snakes woke up seasonally—but were then hacked to death by a Man with the Sling Blade: a pole with a steel curve underneath; from the two ends of that hung a straight double-edged blade (serrated on each side). It cut through brush too tough for a lawn mower.

The unruly undergrowth—before it was cut back—caught my imagination, as the fact that one of my bedroom windows made it possible to step out onto the rooftop did not.

I had never decided to be a writer. It was as if I'd always known. I wrote—first—a book of poetry at seven. I would sit upstairs in my bedroom, backed by wallpaper with green and gray flecks. In the corner panels, a wild jungle scene. And write. I remember in particular one day when school was just out. On the sidewalk a few feet from home, with the Tarzan vines to my right, holding my poetry book, I suddenly had this transfixing experience. My atten-tion turned inward. A mind was thinking inside me. It was not me, but it thought it was. It had absolute certainty about itself, its analysis of the surroundings, that is, my body, my lifetime which it found itself suddenly in, as I watched it wake up and access the situation. Astonished, baffled, it felt, rather knew: "*I am a great writer. Here I am, almost seven years old, and I've nothing to show for it.*"

The little child in me was seared to the core, struck by lightning, a sword blade penetrating my identity. I remember the next thought clearly: "*Mozart was five.*" I was studying little Mozart in piano les-sons. The mind inside me *vowed to catch up.* It was a gut-wrenching experience. I was aware of myself and my lifetime to the ripe age of seven. But also aware of WHO I WAS, and the two didn't match. Myself, the child, observing these thoughts, was imprinted for life— all the while on the opposite end, I would be collecting social scars and trying to protect anyone who cared from knowing about them. I would thus begin in a tangle of knots and also on a very fine, firm foundation.

By age nine in a brown two-ring notebook, I began to print <u>A Nancy Carter Mystery Story</u>, *The Clue on the Jewels*. Having occupied myself not very long before with mud pies, hopscotch, and jump rope, I cast myself, the star sleuth—in a dramatic plot. Chapter I opens: "'Dad,' Nancy called, 'telephone for you.' Jef Carter answered the telephone smiling but as he listened to the telephone his face gradually became sober and solemn":

> As Mr. Carter hung up the telephone receiver his young daughter asked him what was bothering him. "That call I just received was from the two old maids that live about a mile outside of town. They say I must have the case they gave me only yesterday cleared up by the end of this week so they can have the case cleared up before they go to New York. That would be easy to do if I had the time to follow up clues but I have two cases in court the [*sic*] week so I won't have time to work on this case. Those two old maids always gossip so if I turn back their case now, they would do their best to ruin my reputation and they would probably succeed in doing so," explained Mr. Carter. Silence followed for a moment. Then suddenly Nancy let out a scream of delight. "Dad, I have a simply marvolus [*sic*] idea," explained Nancy.

The solution: Yours truly will run down clues. The mystery breaks off after sixty-four hand-printed pages, when fresh out of the hospital, eavesdropping intrepidly outside an open window, Nancy hears, "Okay. I called this meeting because that Carter girl is getting too nosy for her own good and it's time sobody [*sic*] should do something about it."

It was by about the third grade that realizing I was gullible, the most popular girls began to trick me. For instance, sunbathing at Camp Leach—beet red, with a jar of Noxzema in hand—I was teased with (and believed) the horrific information that if you rubbed Noxzema on freckles it caused cancer. I had freckles everywhere. Also, at the camp I astonished myself by impulsively stealing brownies. When my victim told the counselor, I was mortified—with visions of public scorn, perhaps revealing some huge flaw in my nature. What happened next was baffling. I went out into the sparse woods around the cabins, to contemplate my desperate plight, and felt a splintering pain. A heart attack, for sure, I thought. Literally almost paralyzed, I nevertheless struggled to the infirmary. Immediately packed off to my family doctor, I sat in his office as he diagnosed appendicitis. He was going to operate, he said, then punched my stomach one last time. The pain disappeared—about at the sound of "operate." I did not make this up or consciously control it. He then diagnosed malaria and prescribed quinine. My mother drove me back to camp—in a car loaded with gifts, books with paper doll cut-outs, and so forth. But I knew it wouldn't help.

I obeyed my parents, observing ruefully the social consequences. At a sixth-grade party we discovered "Spin the Bottle." A boy had to figure out what comic book you were thinking of to kiss you. Wow! Enchanting. But I dutifully told my mother. She insisted I not play. So, afterwards, I played but ingeniously kept in mind the obscurest of titles—*Beany*—which no one guessed.

One afternoon, the most popular kids were at my home and my guard was down. They saw remnants of my father's shaving whiskers in the sink. Surely they came from his nose, one exclaimed. From this they contrived the nickname "Bugger." Aghast, I craftily managed to switch the term to myself, to carry with horror. But rather that than that my father suffer such an indignity. It was a successful deflection—*in the zone*—though he never heard of the incident.

I separated these events from the writer, who was not touched by them—whose interests were so far from these that that part of me was as if a separate person too aloof to protect *me* in society. This writer me would write for hours, in abstract understanding of the grown-up psychology, so that adults—I later learned—thought I was a grown-up child. I would read the pages aloud to family or friend. To a part of me in this very real inner world, all the rest never happened to "him." I think of this writing part as masculine.

Meanwhile, I achieved my ambition to be a majorette—with kerosene flaming from both ends of the baton, throwing it high in the night sky. I adored twirling finger by finger; the cartwheels, the parades.

I barely made it into Duke because to the admissions committee my journalism and home economics looked like crip courses. No physics or chemistry. The interviewer feared I'd flunk out. But I had a very high SAT score and was a Merit Scholarship finalist. How could that be? I explained that the journalism classes were required for me as editor. We were even at the printer's while the presses rolled. Our paper won a first-place national feature-articles award from the School of Journalism, Columbia University—because of which our small-town selves went to New York to a splashy banquet. I considered journalism a substitute for my big book, which still eluded me at eighteen (irony intended).

I remember arriving at Duke for the academic year with a rash: pink all over—from fear. The rash left, once I got settled in Brown House dorm. In fact, in this new world many past minuses were a plus.

I signed on with the Duke *Chronicle* and, notably in 1960, interviewed the staff of J. B. Rhine, a pioneer in laboratory parapsychology (ESP and PK, mind through matter). Later Rhine asked me to pose for an encyclopedia, a photo that traveled the world. As we stood beside a spinning wire cage he pretended to grade my ability to influence which face of the falling dice turned up when the cage stopped. That would be PK, psychokinesis. (Rhine had a hunch that what gamblers sensed on a roll was real.)

Not long afterwards—keen on Rhine's research—the writer Arthur Koestler flew in from England. Koestler had just published *The Sleepwalkers: A History of Man's Changing Vision of the Universe.* He was to write: Rhine's "burly figure, his broad, open face, his obvious and disarming sincerity, made me think of a woodcutter."[3]

At the West Campus soda shop the Student Union organizers invited him to participate in a discussion. Finding the 259–300 students abysmally uninformed and ignorantly critical, Koestler stomped out. Afterwards, I wrote him requesting a quote for my next *Chronicle* piece and included praise for Rhine. Koestler answered me. And at the same time forwarded my letter—to Rhine! That sealed our relationship.

By senior year I would graduate magna cum laude (Honors and Distinction in History). The book-length honors paper required, Dr. Harold Parker explained, research in an untranslated language. For it to double in my Chinese history class, I must see China through the eyes of an English-speaking author. I chose Pearl Buck. To go to the source, I traveled to her snowed-in Pennsylvania estate. Though all my money was pilfered at a New York subway station, that was incidental compared to a predicament close to home.

The paper needed approval of both Parker and my flaming, fiery-haired Chinese history teacher, who seemed to me almost a Mao Communist. Approving the content, he demanded I write without flair, on the order of "subject verb subject verb." By contrast, Parker was individualistic. He'd grown up around the famous philosopher John Dewey and psychologist Edward L. Thorndike. For the matter to be refereed, I was to meet the well-known literature critic William Blackburn, under whom I'd never had a class because my major was history. I stood by while he read a bit. Then as I trembled to hear the verdict he looked up and uttered the most strange words: *"We can't have a John Donne living today."*

Who was Donne?! The buildup had been so tense I burst into tears. Not that I knew the metaphysical poets or the style of dazzling word play and conceits—the use of farfetched comparisons. Or that he had famously written "No man is an island" and "never send to know for whom the bell tolls; It tolls for *thee*." I was not to see Blackburn again. But Parker went along reluctantly. Later he said he did not like to contradict a colleague but in this case, he thought the advice was wrong and the paper *better the first time, in my own style.*

Meanwhile, the last summer before graduate school, I would sit in our Island View Shores cottage on the Pamlico River. Fresh from waterskiing, nestled in nature, I did the required corrections but sneaked in a few images, telltale signs that it was myself who was the author. And anyone looking through it later would detect the clues in these few brief imagistic passages that in the following pages were snubbed out.

Going to Columbia University with a history major to get a Master of Arts in literature was challenging.

I'd opted out of a part-scholarship at the University of Chicago. Armed with a speed-reading course, I audited or signed up for every literature course in sight. We were graded *only* on required subjects *in a final exam.* That and a two-hundred-page thesis. My seminar leader, the poet John Unterecker, vigorously supported my topic, "spots in Faulkner as in 'Spotted Horses.'" The thesis was *Marking Time with Faulkner.* I had William Faulkner's birthday.

A few months after Faulkner's death (July '62), I flew to his fictitious Yoknapatawpha County (Oxford, Mississippi) to look at his Greek Revival home, Rowan Oak, and his rugged writing cabin with an ox-drawn plow in the field. I interviewed his brother John and a hunting friend who cooked in iron pots in a fireplace.

At Ole Miss, in Oxford, civil-rights activist James Meredith was testing the 1954 *Brown v. Board of Education* decision that in public education "the doctrine of 'separate but equal' has no place." Under a U. S. Supreme Court order, Meredith had become the first black student to register there, having begun classes October 1. But riots broke out, and President John F Kennedy sent in federal marshals to support the 70th Army Engineer Combat Battalion from Ft Campbell, Kentucky, and military police.

It happened that hitchhiking from Ole Miss to my hotel, I rode with two narcotics agents—reassigned to guard Meredith undercover. For whatever reason, they decided to trust me. Unburdening themselves, they confessed to feeling the pressures that came from making false friendships with students instead of drug traffickers. They felt relieved to talk to someone. Conspicuously cracking their door, they said that by a Mississippi law still on the books they could be arrested *if in a hotel room with a woman with the door closed.* And local authorities were looking for an excuse to arrest them. Armed with note cards for my thesis in a large hatbox, I returned by train to New York.

Columbia University had a stellar literature department. Moses Hadas was, said the *New York Herald Tribune*, "one of the world's most distinguished classical scholars."[4] A rabbi, the chairman of the Greek and Latin department, he'd edited or translated many famous ancient Greek tragedians and comedians, Seneca, and others. In the spring of 1963 he sent me a note to come to his office. Not many students spoke in his class. I'd never uttered a word. This next part, I recall vividly—one of those flashes of memory that sticks like to flypaper.

It was raining. To play down my femininity, I exchanged my characteristic tiny-heel pumps for flats. He said he'd observed me in class. He was to teach a pilot Ford Foundation course—"Great Ideas in Antiquity"—remotely, via a telephone and a widescreen broadcast into auditoriums in the segregated Deep South. Would I monitor on site? There'd be five hundred students in four all-black schools: Jackson State and Tougaloo College (Jackson, Mississippi); Southern University and A&M College and Grambling College (Baton Rouge, Louisiana).

It meant postponing my Columbia graduation. Hadas did not anticipate danger but said I must get my parents' consent; he had a hunch about me—"And if I am wrong, at least they can enjoy looking at you." It was the first indication that this elegant professor, later President Pro Tem of the university, with his medium-cropped white beard, who recited Greek in class, was an intuitive.

Naturally I agreed. JFK's assassination was a few months ahead. Martin Luther King Jr.'s assassination four years. With the initial lecture relayed by satellite, the *Tribune* headlined: COLUMBIA TO TELSTAR TO MISSISSIPPI NEGROES (May 31, '63). On Friday, July 19, *Time* ran the story "Teaching: Lectures on the Phone," in which it stated: "A segregationist Mississippi law forbids Negro state colleges to hire white teachers. Last week Moses Hadas, the famed Columbia University classicist, slipped around the law without ever leaving Manhattan."[5]

I was inside the Deep South. Some cabbies refused to drive me into "colored" town. Once a taxi I was in dodged a hailstorm of stones. Looking in on a political rally, I casually told someone what I was doing. He urged me to keep silent: there were people here "*who would kill you if they found out*." But as I reported to Hadas, if he came down, he'd be greeted with a ticker tape parade.

Having missed the university exams, I had to wait for the next round. My seminar advisor suggested that in the interim he recommend me to literary agent John V. Schaffner and his wife Perdita, who were looking for an *au pair* to their four children. Perdita's mother was the Imagist poet Hilda Doolittle, H. D., the sometime fiancé of Ezra Pound. In Freudian analysis she'd fascinated the great Freud, who confirmed her bisexuality. From birth Perdita had mingled with the literati in London and Switzerland. Biographers speculated that her father might be Pound or D. H. Lawrence, her close friend.

When I moved into their century-old, comfy several-story house on East Fifty-third Street, their intense, dark-eyed, dark-haired nine-year-old Nicholas was visiting Pound—THE Pound—in England. He flew back transatlantic alone.

A few months later, ending that enjoyable interlude, I moved in with graduate students the last month before exams. I graduated with a "two." No thanks to the exams. But instead of feeling relief, many of us, surfeited from bleary-eyed nonstop cramming till 5:00 a.m. each morning that last month, rebelled against academics. I applied to the Fifth Avenue Barbizon modeling school and was elated at being accepted, though with my body type I was restricted to sportswear.

But I never went back. My glamour pole spotted a receptionist opening at the Manhattan office of the famed Louis Shurr theatrical agency. It had represented such celebrities as Cole Porter, Ginger Rogers, and Bob Hope. Pleading with Louis's high-powered brother

Lester, who ran the branch, I convinced this one-man show I'd observe the old-fashioned phone system in Johnson Hall, my dorm, whereby the receptionist plugged lines into dozens of holes—though his operated off a single phone (with a multitude of buttons)—and start work the next day.

By mutual consent I was out in six weeks, the last straw being my spastic performance with a top Vegas businessman, like the Sands's Jack Entratter. Weeks after his heart attack, I had him racing room to room, trying to catch up with a call as I kept switching the line from office to office.

But through Shurr, I discovered his sister Gertrude and the Gertrude Shurr–May O'Donnell modern dance studio. Also, during a snowy lunchtime break I rented a Bleecker Street brownstone flat in fabled Greenwich Village west of Sheridan Square; a single room divided by an arch, which split the kitchen off from the living room bedroom, plus a humongous closet.

Gertrude and May, sixty-two and fifty-nine, were early Martha Graham dancers. May—a breathtaking teacher—was the former touring partner of legendary José Limon. May and Gertrude's students had included Gerald Arpino and Robert Joffrey, the Joffrey Ballet founders. They taught on a wooden floor in a studio that overlooked Fifth Avenue. In her seventies May would become quite famous for her pioneering choreographer and dance troupe. I took several years of their instruction—soaking in the confidence and joy they radiated and for the only time in my life building very strong thigh muscles and back arch.

In the span of three months I galloped from my unpursued modeling career past my receptionist sortie to reporter. I literally knocked on the door at United Feature Syndicate and presented my scrapbook of stories. This time declared overqualified, I was hired as editorial assistant under the two male editors.

It was blissful to be in the bohemian Village. Interesting people at every step. Electricity in the air. I never knew what was about to happen—in a bookstore, in the Sheridan Square deli. I thrived on it.

Walking down the street one day, with my ever longer red hair turned under at the ends, the front side-parted, falling almost over one eye in the Veronica Lake style, I was stopped by a professional photographer. At a shoot he gave me a handheld dryer, to make my (freshly washed) hair windblown. For payment, I could take the photos or, if memory serves, $60. Once, I chose the photos; then the money. The second time, comfortable before the camera, I posed in leotards. To relax beforehand, I was offered a vibrating massage gadget (I didn't use it). But mesmerized by the camera, I realized how easy it would be to forget what I was wearing. In fact, is that the glimpse of a towel wrapped around my chest in one of the three head-to-shoulder shots? Yes, in one there's the suggestion of where a towel begins.

I still had not started my "big book." It was in the back of my mind at all times. But I'd no idea what to write, and sitting down asking it to materialize, I drew a blank.

I did not fling myself into wild New York City life. The pill was barely in circulation, and AIDS did not exist, insofar as anyone knew. I was still a virgin.

However, I had any number of boyfriends.

One night I exited the Sheridan Square subway around 10:00 p.m. at the same time as an attractive 5 foot 10 male with hair a deer's-fur blond, and we started to talk. We'd unknowingly attended the same event. I had a press pass from UFS. His was from the counterculture WBAI radio, but he was also a political speech writer and sometime actor in Second City. Becoming the girlfriend of this man I will call Lawrence, I was introduced into a circle of eccentrics and artists at the Village home of "mad millionaire" Marshall Allen. In the living room writers, painters, jazz-saxophone icon Charlie "Bird" Parker's arranger—people of all ethnic backgrounds—mingled in sight of a mountainous bowl of pot. With no pressure to indulge, I didn't but enjoyed the milieu. At Thanksgiving they used an Alice Toklas recipe for turkey stuffing laced with marijuana.

Now came the big day. With Lawrence at twenty-four, I lost my virginity. Very late by New York standards. But I had pondered it long and hard—finally realizing I might never marry.

I was not seduced. Weighing everything, I decided this in fact was to be the very night. However, things did not go as planned. I'd never had a drug. In his apartment I accepted a single whiff of "an ami" (that's what I heard, but it was probably Amyl nitrate). And embarrassingly lost awareness of being in my body. I seemed to travel far away with a conscious Little Dot. Not at all frightened, I was transfixed by its determination, its sacred mission (though I could not see what that was), merged with its destiny, with what *it knew*—in an intense conviction. Everything else fell by the wayside. I was aware only of this journey of my consciousness away from the room, with the Little Dot.

Naturally, this was not the plan in giving me the whiff of the euphoric sex enhancer, precipitating what I now recognize (but did not then) was an OBE, or out-of-body trip. During the OBE the sexual scene went on without "me." For a second (expanded in the mind) as I came back into the room I experienced the sense of climbing *up from underwater*. In that second I said the first name that came to mind, which wasn't "Lawrence." It was not diplomatic. But he wasn't irretrievably consternated. And the relationship, though wobbly, survived. I felt that if on his part it might be as the song said, "But though I'll never love you, we'll sing in the sunshine, we'll laugh every da-ay-ay-ay," I'd take it.[6]

But the Little Dot experience lingered. I groped to find the meaning. I believed immediately in the existence of this window in dimensions. Was the Little Dot my soul? If so, I'd had a glimpse of her behind the scenes, offering me a sacred vision of total commitment but to what?—reaching me to the core.

Once as I left Marshall Allen's house he handed me two joints ("Take these for your dreams"). In my apartment I puffed one of them. Next a mass of stars twinkled *on my eyelids*. Panicked, I opened my eyes. When I tentatively dared to close them, the stars still spread out over a vast sky as if right there. I fought to clear my vision, panicked at feeling a pulsing map of stars bearing down on my eyes. They seemed entirely real. *What did it mean to have stars pulse over your lids?*

I lasted nine months at United Feature Syndicate, then quit. No matter how the editors backed me, their boss would not promote women. And $75.00 a week (what I think my salary was) would barely cover living expenses, including $125 a month (what I think my rent-controlled apartment went for). I began to look for a job copy editing, but when none was forthcoming sublet my apartment for four months in Europe.

We crossed the Atlantic to Le Havre on the coast of France, with many warnings coming my way: *that I would be lonely, that women did not travel solitarily in Europe in 1965.* I became petrified till the first moment I put my foot ashore. All the warnings forgotten, I felt expansive, joyful. France enchanted me. I was in bliss. I could go to the cafés in Montparnasse where Hemingway and Fitzgerald had sat and start my book.

PART TWO

2

March in Paris

Three major influences in my life have passed on, three human beings who shaped my consciousness and memories—all in the same way: remolding, exemplifying a handful of unusual, hard-to-find traits in the Book of Life. I knew all three while in New York City in the mid-to-late '60s. That coincidence is phenomenal when I reflect back now. Even more phenomenal is the first meeting. These experiences changed everything, these expressions of authenticity come to say a few personal words of encouragement about—being Yourself. The variety, the oddity, the unexpectedness is to be not shunned but looked into. For there you will *find what nobody else knows.* That, you can say vocally to the planet with a loudspeaker. That, you will be thanked for. And don't worry if you make a few mistakes.

I was twenty-five years old—in Paris to start my book.

> When young writers came to Paris for the first time, they dropped their luggage at a hotel on the Left Bank and went straight to the Dôme, in hope of meeting friends who had preceded them. Either way they met the friends or else they made new ones.[7]

Just before sailing, I watched Charlie Chaplin in *Limelight.* In a climactic scene a ballerina would not go on stage till forcibly pushed. As Chaplin, a tramp clown, slapped her onto the stage, I felt it was I who got slapped. I got shoved on stage by the tramp clown.

Now I sat intently in Montparnasse cafés (Le Select, Le Dôme, La Coupole, Le Rotunde). In La Closerie des Lilas, Fitzgerald gave Hemingway *The Great Gatsby* and Hemingway penned much of *The Sun Also Rises.*

I roomed at a Left Bank student center on Boulevard St. Michelle. Later I moved into the last home of Oscar Wilde—Hôtel d'Alsace, 13 Rue des Beaux-Arts, St. Germain-des-Prés.

I had not the slightest idea of the book topic. I knew the expected quality but not the content. When I found my characters, they would tell me.

Every morning I sat down at my (nonportable) Underwood typewriter that I'd lugged across the ocean; I broke at brunchtime for a cheese omelet or sidewalk croque monsieur. I breathed in the air, the museums, nearby Notre Dame de Paris cathedral; at some point I'd wind up in Montparnasse like impoverished expatriate artists of the 1920s and '30s, who lived in unheated rooms without running water. I envisaged Gertrude Stein's Lost Generation—though in fact Sartre, Simone de Beauvoir, Picasso, Miró, Max Ernst, Matisse, Dalí, Russian dancers, cinematographers, Kiki the Queen of Montparnasse, to mention a few, also sat in these exact seats. I was not yet aware that Milton Klonsky too, whom I'd not met, had been in Paris just like that.

Perhaps to a lot of people the experience at seven (of the stranger thinking inside me) would have been a childish, long-forgotten hallucination, but it had been far too powerful and startling. Besides, the fact that I'd never told a soul aided its ability (intact, never observed or thought of by anyone but myself) to stay alive. At last came a scene, a signal—a *trigger to begin the book.*

It came from a ragtag beggar crouched outside the Montparnasse bar-café Le Dôme. A crinkled, yellowed sheet of paper dated March 22, 1965, miraculously resurfaced in 2011: "The window was a little dirty, but one could easily comprehend the frenzy of the gestures as the man outside the café drew his fingers to and from his lips, sucking deeply on the imaginary cigarette. Over his shoulder hung a bulging satchel with a wine bottle sticking out of the top. Evidently there was plenty of food inside the satchel, perhaps a loaf of bread."

The story grew in my mind. I imagined he'd had money to buy a meal and then realized he had no cigarette and had exhausted his funds: "His stomach lacked nothing. Yet he must walk away disappointed. All the energy bursting out of the food into its delighted, goring recipient must now go into an urgent walk down numerous streets . . . No one in the past two hours had responded to his open hand. He showed his face against the glass door of the café house, his gestures wilder and wilder, the gentleman diner having turned beggar at last making the final necessary metamorphosis into actor. Facial muscles strained. Lips protruded further, sucking with increasing exaggeration until they seemed to inflate an imaginary balloon." It went on:

> The young woman sitting alone at the table nearest the window debated her reaction. . . .
>
> She did not fear the ordinary. She walked slowly in darkness, never locked a door, kept her unmarked face free of all symptoms of strain in the presence of big dangers. . . . To speak truly, the most striking thing about her was this complete lack of blemishes, complete to the extent of banning even a single bump or stray hair.

The information boinged down into some secret *translation room*. I felt riveted. He saw I noticed. Our two stares met—his face heavily etched with lines like the record of a lie detector, mine blank.

Yet another alert, a *petite madeleine* dunked in tea, triggered the beginning of Proust's *Remembrance of Things Past*. Taste, smell, gesture sent his mind on a voyage, retrieving a forgotten memory. I did not interact with the beggar further except that in dreams and word play I advanced the image. In actual fact, I could not have given him a cigarette even had I wanted to; I had none in my pocket. And my only interest in him was this imaginary trip he triggered—the signal to begin writing right at that spot.

So that day at Montparnasse, I received snatches of pieces of the book, which had meanings deeper than I knew.

I found my first character as—to conserve money—he sat up sleepless all night in a café. Alternate nights he slept in a hotel. He was a Scotsman, Ian Wilson. What fascinated me was his tale of how he broke up with his girlfriend. This was less plot than the core of a character. Ian instigated the breakup by slamming down the phone, making the sound all the louder to silence his emotions, which wanted desperately to call her back. It was intriguing to me to get inside this male's mind. Later I realized Ian could have stepped right out of Søren Kierkegaard's biography, in the sense that Kierkegaard, hiding his feelings, likewise rebuffed the very woman he cared about the most—in his case because his soul, he told himself in anguish, had other plans.

Also memorable was Paris by Night, when in the middle of nowhere I got separated from the tour alongside a distinguished-looking middle-aged Italian, whereupon he confessed it was in seeing me he signed up. Did I want to see a *real* Paris by Night?

We went to the Lido, then a password-protected entrance on a street. I had no idea it was a fancy prostitution house. Still with utmost courtesy, he asked for two women (clients chose any combination). And we went into a private room. There was no way out but I didn't feel danger. Then a young woman, looking vulnerable, I thought, asked me, "*Voulez-vous participer?*" ("Do you want to participate?") I said no.

Locked out of my student lodging, I stayed with the elegant Italian—the owner of a Milan Ferrari dealership, who for years had had no vacation—in the fancy Hotel George V in a giant bed, during which nothing at all happened, because he was a gentleman.

The book begun, and one month already past, having wiggled through experiences as a woman traveling alone, I regretfully dragged myself away from Paris to see more of Europe. Who knew when I'd be back here. I had bought a Eurail pass to ride free across the continent: Paris to Spain, Italy, Greece, and Scandinavia, possibly spending some nights on the train; other nights, I would find lodging with my *Europe on $5 a Day*. Just because I adored Paris didn't mean I wouldn't adore those cities as well.

As I headed down through Spain I managed to get help in lifting the office-sized unwieldy Underwood typewriter through the window. Things were relatively smooth in Madrid, Toledo, Seville, and Granada. In southern Spain I hooked up (not romantically) with a young guy who was headed down into Morocco; I thought why not tag along, but he left just after we crossed the border of Morocco into Fez.

What female—long haired, lugging a heavy typewriter—would travel alone pre–hippie invasion? Hustlers with street cred could not make sense of it. Luckily I found a wonderful guide in Fez who brought the history alive. For the next stop, the long ride to bustling Marrakech, he introduced me to a Moroccan Cook's Tour guide, whom, he proudly said, had a PhD. I could travel free. After the good fortune of being squired around by the illiterate Fez guide, I was horrified in the bus to find the other guide making advances.

This background preconditioned one of the three Big Meetings.

Jean-Marie Mensaert

My first ambition was to be an architect.

Slide: Opening

Slides: Corridor 2 / Ruins

3

Meeting Jean-Marie (Jan) Mensaert

I'm unique.
But then everyone's unique.
They just take the first scrap
that comes along
—Jan Mensaert

After dark the bus pulled in at the fabled La Mamounia hotel in Marrakech, built in the palace of an Alaouite prince. I was in for a shock. It being the end of a religious holiday, the desk clerk assured me that the whole town was booked full. Would I prefer the frightening experience of sharing the room with a man who leered at me like at a prostitute or to be tossed into the street? I was terrified of being cooped up with him—locked in with a man whose intentions were all too clear—but what to do? Taking the alternative I judged the least risky, I chose the room.

Fortunately, he spent most of the night carousing at the bar while I fretted lest he return. When he did, he collapsed into snoring. I huddled on my edge of the bed, vigilantly awake, not getting a wink of sleep.

Obviously inept in an exotic Berber city, I hurried out at 6:30 a.m., *determined to find a friend*. I was used to light risk, but here, I realized, I could not make myself understood, my usual tactics would hold no sway whatsoever. I would not be protected by the attacker. I'd even hitchhiked in Fez with a man who put a rifle in the front seat between us, just in case I was dangerous. But *this* guy was deaf.

Founded by a Sahara desert tribal leader, Youssef Ben Tachfine, the High Atlas-backed town of Marrakech once ruled an empire from Castile (Spain) to the Sudan. A French protectorate in the early twentieth century, it regained its freedom in 1956. Lined by orange trees, Avenue Mohammed V leads from the European district to the old walled city, the medina—with its red-colored buildings, winding passages, and labyrinths. I hurried to the medina. In the *souk* (or markets) leather goods and other wares hung from open shop doorways or were piled in front—on streets too narrow for cars.

Slide: A Moroccan Souk

The main square is magical, bustling Djemma el Fna, known for its snake charmers and acrobats.

A popular coffeehouse overlooking Djemma el Fna, the Café de France had an upper- and a ground-level terrace. Except for one cup of coffee, the lower terrace showed no sign of life. Scanning the jalabas inside, I saw that no one would suit my purposes. So I sat beside the full cup and waited.

Not long afterwards a tall, excessively thin European twenty-eight-year-old strode lankily to the table—his short sandy blond hair combed loosely to one side, all that was left of a formerly James Dean hairdo. He wore tinted prescription glasses. His legs moved nimbly, his feet solid on the ground. That was Jean-Marie Mensaert. Claiming the coffee, he sank his head in his newspaper, *Le Monde* (the *World*). I asked to borrow a page.

Jean-Marie taught French in high school in Larache, a formerly Spanish Moroccan village near Tangier in the North. As his native land, Belgium, had two languages, his Flemish name was Jan. Despite his pixie smile and command of any subject, he'd spent the previous night in a hashish den, where, being broke, he gambled for bus fare home.

Hard to beat when he put his mind to anything, he won. But a hundred percent convinced no European could beat Moroccans at cards, his traveling companion Moulay bet against him. Thus, they came out even. This parallel ordeal set the stage for him to be out at the crack of dawn.

I would later dub him a man with *too much imagination*. Along with dignity. Refinement. He would show me the intricacies of Marrakech—his inventiveness never being at a loss for something to imagine; wrap with sparkling possibility, true or not.

Jean Mensaert arrived in Morocco, having taught himself "Scheherazade" on the piano at fourteen and repeatedly devoured the *Tales from a Thousand and One Nights*. Attracted to the Orient, he hitchhiked at twenty from Belgium through Bangkok, Burma, Malaysia, Indonesia, and the Far East, undertaking the trip with

pennies—not spending those. Among the colorful stories he was glad
to recite, he slept on cold temple floors and begged outside bakeries
for stale bread and crusts. To add the dimension of art to everything
(into a conversation, for instance) intrigued him. Anything done in-
artistically, he ignored.

He did not feel at home in the West with its materialistic out-
look. In Morocco, "the thinking man's country," he did.

Some years later, with details more accurate than I could sum-
mon today, I described him as "the most original person I've ever met
and maybe the saddest and the biggest comedian." I warmed to his
wry British look and "the funny vertical wrinkles continuing the lines
at the top of his nose." He was slim, a bit frail looking. His attention
on his Paris newspaper, I surprised him by addressing him first. My
account continued:

> An hour afterwards we were in a garden, from which incident
> he would later concoct in a novel a scene between himself
> and the love of his life Aziza, in which "you had your part,
> as a little princess taking me up on the platform of the now
> ruined palace of her father, showing me Marrakech in the
> distance and laughing at my unwillingness to admit that this
> is not a time-stand-still place where Aziza and I can dwell
> forever, having dreams and unreality for domesticity."
> And then it developed that everything that was touched
> by this man became a story; that I was no longer me, that
> everything that occurred thereafter was lived by characters.[8]

Still without funds, he secured bus tickets to Larache for the three
of us—himself, Moulay, and me—by inviting along a rich Moroccan
son of a pasha (provincial governor).

The coastal fishing village in which Jean-Marie lived was right on
the Atlantic, a few kilometers from the unguarded Roman ruins of

Lixus (a Phoenician trading post founded in the seventh century BC, called by some Greek writers the Garden of the Hesperides, site of one of Hercules' labors). Larache being a former Spanish protectorate, many whitewashed houses had blue doors and shutters, and Spanish balconies. Behind ornate iron grilles luxuriant potted plants and flowers overhung the walls. We walked past potholes in an unpaved street to his corner house.

Slide: Alley (Morocco)

I wasn't prepared for the sight, once he flung open the door.

There was the typical glazed-ceramic wall and floor tile. And an inner courtyard—a rectangular skylit room without a roof.

Jean-Marie's Living Room

Hand-hammered copper and brass (water pitchers, jugs, incense burners) from England, Egypt, and Morocco on tiers of shelves caught my eye. But most unexpected were a hundred classical and Arabic LPs: Um Kulthum to Dvořák to the complete Edith Piaf. The heart-wrenching "If you love me, really love me, let it happen I don't care" (in French) erupted into the room—exactly seeming to reflect Jean-Marie's sentiments, as I would learn. Or Piaf's "No, I regret nothing." In life he'd have a lot to regret if he chose. When the sounds soared, my heart did.

Mozart was the other half of the music picture. Jean-Marie could sing every Mozart aria by heart. Intensity or spontaneity made up for the lack of operatic voice.

This was the good awakening. In the rude one the rapacious-looking pasha's son tried to buy me for a second wife. However, Jean's clean-cut features reassured me. Little did I know how little he valued safety. Unafraid to show what he'd been up to, when he left a room he never concealed the evidence, even leaving the cap off a toothpaste tube. This trait I would like to emulate. He exhibited no sense of shame or fear that another might disapprove, no matter what. Just the contrary, though—it bears repeating—with the charm of a child.

At night I slept in the lone bedroom; in the living room they slept on *catrés* (wooden divans) lining the wall. But I woke abruptly—in great fright—to find the two strong Moroccans muttering Arabic, laughing, over my bed. Not again! Would I be raped??! Belying the scene before my eyes, I felt surely safe with Jean-Marie near. Controlling my sheer panic, in broken French I reminded Moulay of the heavy price to pay if he dared anger Jean. More Arabic. Moulay chuckled. They left.

Fleeing to the tiny bathroom (with the traditional hole to squat over), I locked myself in. Whereupon they woke Jan, to reassure me to come out. I no sooner did than he fell again into a "coma." And though nothing further happened, I dreamed of falling down through darkness with no sides in a bottomless-seeming hole. I would never forget that sense of a fall impossible to break. Nothing to grab onto. I had the sense: *This is forever, there's no way out.* A nightmare. Later, I realized that Moulay was instrumental in the rescue. He'd explained that my Western dress, casualness, and midback-length red hair were normal in my country—not lewd. Oddly, Moroccan hustlers took their cue from some tourists. It would be a mutual education in the years to come; local hustlers learned of drugs such as LSD from tourists, and Westerners used this country to escape prying eyes at home; the impoverished Moroccan "street" willingly accommodated but did not necessarily admire.

I wanted Jean-Marie to evict the guest, which he said customs of hospitality forbade. But that he'd conduct a ceremony to ensure the pasha's son took me as a sister, thus untouchable: the pasha's son was to kiss my forehead. He did, but I felt no safer and was not. None too soon for me but also without further consequence, the intruder left.

All the locals, including Jean-Marie, bought fresh vegetables and meat daily from the market, where just-mortared saffron, cayenne, cinnamon rose in mountains in a stall. Be it with a nutmeg ball or an onion, every meal was made from scratch—except for local sardine and tuna cans. I marveled at the lightning-fast knife slicing to cut parsley, and the use of even the stems; the tasty side salads of minutely cut tomatoes, beets, cucumbers. Few homes (his included) had refrigerators, though in the *souk* some "frigos" were available: imported European motors inside poorly insulated local exteriors. He cooked on charcoal. Dipping bread (hot from a town oven), we ate without utensils.

With no indoor bath, only a toilet, it was customary to take an hour-long weekly shower in town. Or sit on the floor in the steaming *hammam*, Turkish bath. I enjoyed the special stone that eliminated deep dirt; it was said that it got you cleaner once a week than daily baths and showers Western-style.

Slide: Larache (Port)

In easy walking distance—if you ignored or threw stones at the wild dogs—was an unspoiled beach, its wild cliffs marked with caves and colored rock formations. But no respectable female could wander it unaccompanied. Here I liked to imagine the ships from Carthage (Tunis) that had passed.

On a windswept rock overlooking large Atlantic white caps, translating from the Flemish, Jean-Marie read me his poems, fetched out of a trunk.

Then he built a sand tomb in perfect silence—in it burying three dead beetles. He added a long twig walkway. Spellbound, I soon learned that his reconstructions had references, mythological associations. As he entombed the scarab/beetles, was his architect's mind in Egypt? Did he bury the symbol of rebirth, the rising sun? Wordlessly cross the barriers of spoken language with some unhinted-at, un-dreamed-of implications in the psyche—supposing one could take this *dream language* and authenticate it? At the time I was not deci-phering—just, as with the beggar, caught in the silent signing.

He'd first wanted to be an architect; he noted the similarity of his name to that of the great seventeenth-century Jules Hardouin Mansart. At seventeen he tried being a painter; before and after that, a composer; only when traveling did he turn to poetry. Bombarded by one artistic passion, then another, bewildered by choices at an early age, he'd suffered, he said, from lack of discipline: "I had it com-ing at me from all sides."

I watched him paint. Running out of pink, he grabbed a lipstick tube; cigarette ashes for gray. Silent, thoughtful, he drew detailed freehand blueprints of excavations. Then with an arm over his eyes—not to see where the pencil point landed—he made numerous quick thrusts on the paper as in aerial bombing! About life's physicalities he paid little attention. He appeared to hate showers but never smelled. Alternately, never protecting what in himself needed protection—though quick to care for wounded animals. In fact, death defiance was in his fiber.

Woman's Face

Jean-Marie did not yet reveal all this. But much dribbled or exploded out. I was fascinated to be with "the consummate artist." I'd no idea that "Jean" (his French name) and "Jan" (his authorial Flemish name) translated in Scottish as "Ian," my novel's first protagonist.

To reach a closed-up part of his creativity—in writing, not painting or music—he smoked pot. This poetical ability then unblocked. He neglected to tell me of an infant trauma that left scars. Instead, he put forward the light, bright, joyful side. This left me with an impression not so much of depth as of sparkle. If he skated on thin ice, it was with ethereal blades, not heavy.

His subjects were universal: love, death, suffering, a tiny animal. I was very moved by everything: how, when necessary, he used a brush with few bristles. How he disappeared into silence. He was not yet in print. And I advocated he take the scattered sheets in that trunk and contact a publisher. He also loved to tell stories. I was never sure which were invented or embellished.

I literally fled. I forced myself, as with each passing day I felt more lethargic. There was something about the place. I lost all will. But I was impacted by the brilliance of this completely original person. I delayed, thinking each day he might make a move. But he didn't. When I left, he only shook my hand. What formality!? Then I felt its intensity. He suggested I route my itinerary through Belgium, staying with his parents. I agreed. The handshake was as if some giant force moved through me.

I fled, not looking back, glad I could make myself go. As if the longer I stayed, the more I would be sucked into the vegetative atmosphere, the world that had no urgent time sense, no projects that had to be completed, no deadlines, no driving ambition; that was perhaps fatalistic—forgot goals. I had never felt the call of vegetating before. Nature, the trees in my backyard, the forest behind, had always been the setting to write; underground, supportive, not urging static, lethargic surrender to Life as it dealt out experiences inside mass settings, which, while colorful, did feel like a robbery of the Will. Of course, Jean-Marie frequented not the educated Moroccans but "the street." The dream had warned me. I took note. It reflected my sensation of tumbling down forever, endlessly, without the ability to stop the fall.

After Larache I went on to visit a French couple on the Rivera. Here, I got my first taste of a wife's high standing if her job description was household manager.

Then Venice, Florence, Rome; by boat from Brindisi, Italy, to Corfu, Greece, to Athens. Finally the Orient Express to Belgium. Jan had written his parents to "welcome [me] as you've never welcomed anyone before." Then England. And home. However, not to forget the Louvre, the Prado, Spanish exhibits, the cathedrals, the National Museum of Athens. I must pause at Greece.

From Athens, I took a shoestring bus tour of the Peloponnese. At 114 miles from Athens sits Delphi, atop a cliff at the foot of 8,061-foot-high Mount Parnassus. As our bus arrived a departing taxi veered to a sharp halt.

The small hotel was full. But the attractive passenger, spotting me, bribed the manager with cigarettes and whiskey to stay another night. A dashing Englishman in the British Armed Forces at Malta, he said he was on holiday in Delphi to rock climb. He pointed to the vertical mass of rocks. Would I like to go straight up?

Leaving the group on the horizontal footpath to the Temple of Apollo, I took my position below his legs. I was thrilled by the slight danger, the search for hand- and footholds in the lofty slope overlooking gorgeous olive groves—in a mythical location sacred to Apollo and Dionysus. Once, finding nothing else to hold onto, I wrapped my palm around his calf, feeling a sensual jolt.

Delphi was "the naval of the known world." (Legend had it, Zeus released two eagles toward opposite ends of the Earth, and they met there.) At Delphi lived the Oracle of Apollo, the advice "Know thyself."

To hear the echo, he yelled down the mountain—in a Shakespearian voice—the startling words "There's blood upon my hands!"

We climbed down after reaching the ancient stadium of the Panhellenic Games. Then back at ground level sat on a restaurant balcony over ouzo—a bristling excitement in the air. As we looked out at the panorama everything was pitch black—only pinpricks of lights from houses visible on the mountainside. In the distance I heard sheep bells tinkling.

Suddenly two flying streaks of light shot across the sky: two birds, lit up iridescently like fireworks. Then pitch blackness. Then a pair of these inexplicable cometlike fire darts. We watched as the birds penetrated the blackness; then it was dark again, then lit-up birds. Nobody ever explained it to me, but I'm sure there's an explanation. I find only this on the web: that the site of Apollo's oracle was "a slope cupped by towering 900-foot-high cliffs that are known as the Phaedriades, the Shining Ones, because at dawn and twilight they glow with incandescent light, as if they were the translucent crust of some volcanic furnace."[9]

That night we slept on a balcony, and the next morning he told me movingly, though it had been only light romance, not sexual, *"For me, it won't happen again."* I never forgot his name, Harry Hickling. Or that utter surprise and bafflement as we watched the lit birds streak through the pitch-blackness.

I was to experience other times afterwards singular—never-to-be-forgotten—encounters, fleeting, the span of a mere day. That memory of the fiery birds (why pairs?) stuck inside me: a Pythian prophecy transported out of the past. The heightened sense of vision of a silent film. I could not unravel it. But it stamped itself upon my psyche. Soon to meet my main character in New York, I would call him, in the novel, Oracle and say he was Apollonian, as opposed to Dionysian, inspired by this incident, in part.

4

Meeting Milton Klonsky

And the Raven, never flitting, still is sitting, *still* is sitting
On the pallid bust of Pallas just above my chamber door;
And his eyes have all the seeming of a demon's that is dreaming,
And the lamp-light o'er him streaming throws his shadow on the floor;
And my soul from out that shadow that lies floating on the floor
Shall be lifted—nevermore!

—Edgar Allan Poe

There are all those raven people, and I'm not one of them. . . . . Each of us has a self the other owns.

—Milton Klonsky

Back in New York, I found that for Lawrence, the relationship hadn't survived the four-month's trip. This was predictable. On this other level, of important meetings, it was foredoomed. For the next Unrepeatable was close on the scene, barely blocks away.

Ensconced in my old apartment, I was now a Random House copy editor. My own book begun, whomever I met I looked at as a possible character. Bits of many people might figure in.

Next door in another Bleecker Street brownstone was beautiful, thin, elegant, groovy Sarah, the daughter of a black Chicago jazz musician. She was the mistress of Barney Rosset, Grove Press publisher, and would lead me to my main male protagonist. Waging legal wars in the United States on behalf of *Lady Chatterly's Lover* and *Tropic of*

Cancer, publishing Ginsberg's "Howl" and Burrough's *Naked Lunch* along with Beckett's *Waiting for Godot*, to name a few, Rosset, with his Grove Press and *Evergreen Review*, successfully toppled censorship. In "The Most Dangerous Man in Publishing," Louisa Thomas wrote, "He found writers who wanted to break new paths, and then he picked up a sledgehammer to help them whale away at the existing order."[10] More later.

I cultivated Sarah, who occasionally was sent to Paris on business. Rosset told her, she said, "You don't know how to talk." He then taught her. Sometimes I babysat her son. I believed he was Rosset's, though perhaps he wasn't. For my book I confiscated his line "What's a mecent mixer?"

I have to admit that babysitting was a ploy. I hoped through this association to get back with Lawrence. Once again I found myself in a room with a bowl of pot, which she said to help myself to and I didn't. One night Sarah invited me to have a drink at the Corner Bistro. She stopped across the street at 375, to pick up the eccentric Marguerite Young—almost fifty, newly famous for *Miss MacIntosh, My Darling*—whose apartment I remember for the angels hanging from the ceiling. Young had received a Guggenheim and taught at Columbia, the New School, and the Iowa Writers' Workshop.

Walking three abreast—Marguerite Young with short, straight, unglamorous hair, in a long dress with shawls and scarves—we headed out. Marguerite had spent nearly eighteen years on her thousand-plus-page novel. I was to beat that record, though I had no idea of such a prospect. Under other circumstances, this chapter would recall my unforgettable evening with Young. But that was wiped from memory by what happened next.

I met Milton Klonsky down the street from where I lived—sometime round about late November 1965 (near his forty-fifth birthday)—in a small West Village bar, the Corner Bistro. I didn't make any connection then with the Café du Dôme, where the book-writing for THE series he was to star in started, triggered by a gripping kinetic symbol "on the move," a beggar who momentarily caught me squarely in the eye, *where I alone* (which was to be a theme) even noticed his miming. No connection except that Milton's face too was filled with wrinkles of experience, folds of secret knowledge—not esoteric but doled out by a full (or overfull) life.

I met him in a bistro. That term was Russian, meaning "hurry up, be quick."

There he sat in a dark, smoky, narrow interior—alone. Perhaps this was the small viewing position (round in the mind's eye) that was to hold a square peg. Or he was the square peg sitting in dim light at the rectangular booth, having mastered this impossible task of putting a square peg in a round hole, which of course is exact. He had, just as the street he lived on was on West Fourth just where—with no extension at all but coming to a point—it intersected West Eleventh. Sarah made a beeline for him in the back. It was clear she admired him greatly—his intellect, his stature, his hipster quality even cooler than her slinky sophistication, unthrown by it, unintimidated—and I stared into his hypnotic eyes.

I instantly recognized his presence, and without understanding what had happened, shot into a vibration, magnetized by his words and eyes. I did not feel a physical attraction. I felt something stronger that superseded any ability to feel outside it, *huge, welling up, spreading like a widening full-circle ripple, which is what the present does when it incorporates larger amounts of time.* I descended into a deep pool, a beautiful void or vortex. I did not know that then. I only felt absorbed by the largeness, the impact of being nailed to the stake on the spot, in the situation I was in, which was *being introduced to a powerful force that emitted its own frequency.* That potential I did not know about took over: resonance. I was carried, as surely as Lois Lane by Superman, upward, in this case to his vibration. It was so natural seeming.

Milton Klonsky

I was transported and felt at ease yet transfixed, wherever it was we went. Time and space opened, and we "fell into" wherever this vibration was. Where we went was into understanding, recognition, sudden insight—he using his voice exclusively for insight as if forbidden not to, and which I received, somehow mastering on the instant the ability to decode his crypticness.

He was older by nineteen years. And his wisdom, his breadth, were well informed. He was not discovering himself. He knew who he was. No one else that I'd met so covered this stretch of what a human could be in one container from logic to mysticism, "the street" to erudite and ineffable ends alike. Of Russian Jewish ancestry, he had a swarthy Mediterranean coloring and somewhat stocky build with black hair graying wavily. Beat essayist Seymour Krim described the "inhuman guns . . . great eyes, green-grey, catlike, opaque, the possessors of some secret knowledge of mystery which later reminded me almost exactly of the hypnotizing eyes we see in photographs of Rimbaud."[11]

Born on Staten Island in 1921, Milton relocated quickly, "going"—he put it—"from apartment to apartment and block to block, cubicles within cubes, all over the Mondrian grid of Greater New York." This move from countryside to city, which affected him not only psychologically but metaphysically, created, he said, a "breach . . . as wide and deep as that which supposedly separates naturalist and Platonist." Why? Because the city's abstract geometry influenced him in one direction, the messy, disorderly countryside another.[12]

Perhaps it was (I think so) the very first evening he invited me to Fire Island on the weekend, the "in" beach south of Long Island; Marshall Allen had a large guest wing there .

I said yes. I was not committing to anything and could easily (I thought) keep the relationship slow burning. Leaving the ferry, I feasted on the sight: friends charging cornucopias of seafood including lobster to Marshall's tab for delivery.

Milton said to me in our bedroom that night he was palimpsestuous. I was at the one extreme attracted to the extent of worshipping everything he said. On the other, not keen on our encounter becoming a down-on-the-ground relationship. In fact, I felt a desire to run in the other direction when he kissed me . . . too moist feeling, heavy handed. Would my feelings reverse if he were indifferent or didn't cross so determinedly past my boundaries? He said, "I'm not like this with other girls" but was immediately in hot pursuit.

I met Milton, and realized HE was the main character of my book, and that part of my authorial job consisted in taking down his conversation with a female character I identified with, Patsy (later renamed Paula). The book was in the manner of Tolstoy's *War and Peace*—in one sense only: I would counterpoint two couples.*

So I had a main character. I was as if his biographer. As no imagination would in any way reproduce his effect, I would record his words—almost all picture-perfect aphorisms. Like "Write it, *your*

---

* In the earthy couple (Anny and Joseph) Anny's dilemma will be whether she can continue being "the good wife, the salt of the Earth," or whether, meeting the enigmatic Ian, she'll yield to her fascination.

life, as you would *write a novel.*" But not said mildly. It was explosive—an instant knowing, a compact "prediction." He said, "I think we *enact* our lives."

Memorizing—as in my reporter days—I hurriedly left a restaurant table and ran to the toilet to unload on paper my head stash of his words. Collecting me in my apartment, he described it: "roaches running wild like buffalo on the plain, curtains like a coal miner's lungs."

They were burlap. I'd found the furniture abandoned on a street. Villagers often shopped that way. I had no idea that, strapped for cash, he screened unsolicited manuscripts.

We began to see each other practically every night. I had a fine sense of touch and normally would have welcomed his advances. Nineteen years older, he crept the physical part further and further but basically had to reconcile himself to the fact that I didn't fall in love with him sexually.

About my Maginot line in the sand, beyond which he could not go, he quipped, "I feel like George Washington at Valley Forge, and you've kept me here all winter."

Yet for a time I saw no one else. Anyway, you never know what a relationship will turn into (he didn't), but I thought I had it figured out. Keeping him at bay physically was a herculean task with his powers of persuasion. He said, "I'm not one way in love and another in everything else. . . .

"Other men bring out your weakness. *I bring out your strength. . . .* It's *not your will against my will.* It's your will against my need."

As he insisted on pushing our relationship ahead, I had no time to figure out what I really wanted—wonder, "If he didn't persist so much, would *I* run after *him?*" I thought that logically, being a smart guy, he would figure this out, which he did, but it didn't change anything. Why didn't he play hard to get? But something prevented him.

In fact, he was to say early on, "This would have to be either love or despair. It's up to you to choose which."

During evenings he seemed highly industrious, reading thick

books while I copy edited Random House manuscripts in his apartment before going into the Village. About a famous author, he commented on the style: "Dr. Johnson could do that.* This man can't. He's got to get rid of those triptychs." I agreed but could never have stated it that way. He also told me, concentrating the tiny moment out of the huge glob of time and space: "Sometimes you see errors where there are none. You want to give each word its oar to row in on." I could compare that when da Vinci had to paint the faces of Jesus and Judas in *The Last Supper*, according to Giorgio Vasari, he hesitated. He searched. What faces could model these unique expressions? Were there any? So for this character—my teacher, model—my imagination was not so strong as the living experience. He said to me, which I put into my character's mouth: "I don't settle. I *alight*. I'm much more volatile, I'm much more evanescent, I'm much more of a spirit than you can possibly imagine. And all this [the difficulties of our relationship] turns me into *so much more clay*."

I might have pondered hours over these phrases. But in some nonvocal, even mute part of me I knew what he meant. Knew what it was to *alight* with fairy wings, to delicately touch or brush an object and with perfect freedom speed away. Or flick my finger or simply wish it and off it would be. I knew what it was to be evanescent, glowing, invisible. I knew what it was to have such power. I knew what it was, also, to be turned into clay by reality. Me, most of all, could become formless, lose my identity. Why did I know this? Why did I identify with it? Why was he my spokesman, my mouthpiece, where I had no voice and could not speak? Why did he glitter in the dark like a lost or never-known dream, very real, very lived, embodied, exemplified, effective, practical? Or so it seemed—in hearing one such sentence, and there were numbers. In my small office I made a bulletin board. My postings there he called his "raisin sentences"—plump conspicuous passages that caused mouthwatering, which I could not overlook.

Milton spoke in a clipped speech, like Humphrey Bogart, and

---

*Samuel Johnson was a celebrated English literary figure in the eighteenth century; James Boswell recorded his biography in a two-volume *Life of Samuel Johnson*.

wore a trench coat. He chain smoked and was nearsighted, which partly accounted for Krim's first impression that Klonsky, passing him in the courtyard of their apartment building, stared *through* him!—"stoney, rude, the hard-guy." But when they met, Krim said, Klonsky's personality entered his "being—tore through it actually— like a torpedo into the unguarded gut of a battle-innocent smug cruiser. I had never met anyone even remotely like him nor could I have conceived him in my imagination."

Krim admired the "fine and deep mind that was fixed like a rule beyond every flare of mood, behind his furrowed, swarthy face (now Roman-looking, now Jewish, now Spanish)." He found "nothing a hair's width false," though "Klonsky's mind seemed to contain the ENTIRE hip literary-intellectual university and closely grasped with an IQ that could stutter your butter too." However, "at appropriate moments, he electrically bit out the language of the ballpark and streets."[13]

When his look turned inward, I could see he was not impenetrably armored, but vulnerable. Below his bushy eyebrows his intense concentration revealed his private nature; a laugh crackled. If he felt warmth coming his way, he never let it slip by unnoticed. He registered affection the way I pounced on his words. If working out in the gym, he had a flat stomach. This in-the-bodyness was exactly as Krim described: he said, "I got the downhome gooseflesh warning that I was on the way in for the most significant human and intellectual experience of my life up to then.

"I wasn't wrong."[14] *Ditto.*

One evening he said suddenly, "*Play* with me. I can go to any carnival, put on any mask."

This was, again, down-home reality. This glass-sharp sense of the real, this peak-type stimulation that I felt in excitement came from a great writer. And, voilà, he said you could only go as far up as you could go in its opposite direction. But he had "a little boy inside" who told him, "There's some fruit out there, Milton, *that only you can pick.*" Another time he said, "I was *a crazy kid.* . . . You know what I was *crazed **by**, immortality!*" He went on: "Something in me still says, '*Me* die? *I'm* not going to die,' and 'I'm going to be good.'"

Each word packed a wallop. Buried here in brevity were centuries of implication perhaps. Here was the end point, and where was the beginning??? Where was the journey, to arrive at the destination?

So it goes without saying that I listened as he said, "You are probably in love with me—and don't even know it. And will be for a long time."

Was it true? I felt that it was true. What if it were true but that I couldn't do anything about it. Why? Too young? I still wanted not exactly to sew my wild oats. I thought he much more astutely put it, "The problem is I didn't leave room for your imagination. You're such a romantic," he said. "And here I have everything romantic all set up and it doesn't faze you; you think this is ordinary. Other girls find me strange, mysterious, the dark poet, but you find me everyday. Maybe that's the trouble. I didn't leave anything for you to invent. I *invented it all* already.

"You've given me some deep invitation," he said. "I'm not stupid."

Milton was passionate—as he put it, "a shouter." He did not feel things idly, limply. He could not accept that I would not fully, longingly fling myself into a physical affair. But I thought: "apocalips." He quoted Robert Frost about a bird: "The question that he frames in all but words / is what to make of a diminished thing." Why couldn't he take the relationship on *my* terms? Why, indeed. I would have to be very creative, even mercurial, to get through this story alive.

These two meetings and the next were to come in a one-two-three (hits or strikes) scenario. They filled the New York stage with ineffable, deep suspense and happiness. Milton was fairly penniless, as attested to by the sparse number of his sweaters—a scruffy maroon one, a smoky gray—modest corduroy pants, and his apartment furnishings. Sight unseen, he supported my writing.

I had a spiritual couple and an earthy one. The spiritual couple was drawn from life. The earthy one, Anny and Joseph, I made up. Playing the piano with a peculiar passion ("those heavy, labored sounds, rolled with effort off some great key of feeling"), Anny is on a tightrope of disenchantment—married to Joseph. In a fairly strong evolution he begins to realize he is imaginationless—lacking in spontaneity—and that that may be a fault. So he makes efforts to jog himself out of the stereotype.

Disrupting her placid existence, along comes Ian, who is not convinced it's even possible that someone so frank, genuine, unprotected as Anny is not a fraud. He has undisclosed motives, conscious but convoluted, as when internalizing a private struggle he hides his better side.

My Milton character, Robert, wanted "to burn in a magnesium flame—to burn out *but slowly*. Not like the moth at the candle."

He is paired with Patsy—in the published book renamed Paula. Beginning with the format of counterpointed couples from Tolstoy's *War and Peace*, I intended no relationship to the theme *war and peace*. Little did I know.

I was gripped to explore what sprang from the heart? the instincts? the life force? Not instincts as inherited drives but a quality I'd no word for at the time, that meant that you unthinkingly followed something inside. *Could I trust it?* In a stylistic device—Little Chapters—images and symbols also drove the book, stimulating the reader (and myself) to ask why they were there:

Little Chapter

"What do you think of when you think of Apollo?" Paula asked.
"Well, there are a number of things," said Robert.
"But primarily?"
"First of all, clarity. Truth."

"What else?"

"Physical beauty, youth."

"Doesn't that seem a contradiction?"

"Not to me," he said. "DO YOU THINK BEAUTY IS ONLY THE WINDING STAIR?"

The Little Chapters were not explained. I did not say, nor did Milton, that "winding stair" had a source in Yeats. I did not even think the thought, because *his phrases just hit me full blast with unconscious understanding, like a ton of bricks.*

Seymour Krim had edited *The Beats,* introduced Jack Kerouac's *Desolation Angels,* and was currently a reporter for the *New York Herald Tribune.* A friend of Milton's since 1945, he idolized Klonsky in "Two Teachers—Nuts, Two Human Beings!"—in *Views of a Nearsighted Cannoneer.* Mark Cohen, author of *Missing a Beat: The Rants and Regrets of Seymour Krim* (2010), said, "I would not put Krim between Kerouac Canal and Mailer Mountain. Krim is a nonfiction Saul Bellow. His article about the poet Milton Klonsky is Bellow's *Humboldt's Gift* in thirty pages."[15] William Styron called *Views of a Nearsighted Cannoneer* "one of the most profound, truthful, courageously honest forays into the territory of necessary enlightenment that I have ever read" (back cover). In *Namedropping,* Richard Elman termed the book "pathbreaking, the original self-advertisements, but also raunchy and tender and aware." He said Krim's "memoir of his friendship with the writer Milton Klonsky stays with me even now, thirty years after I first read it the first time."[16]

Sy Krim began to call me "Red from Random House." He regretted that he'd rarely recorded Milton's words. I thought that in my exact transcriptions, I might fill that hole.

Of some of his statements to Krim, Milton told me, "I was a sort of charming idiot then, in the way Dostoyevsky's idiot was charming."

He had an unfinished novel, *White Designs*—the title based on the Cabala concept that what was *not* written down in the Bible—*the white around the Hebrew letters*—revealed its deeper meaning.* He'd received an advance, and it was about two decades later. Would he ever finish?

Krim wrote: "As I watched Milton closely during the years of our thickest friendship I saw him silently groaning under the blackest weights of anyone I knew. His loneliness had been trebled by his sense of responsibility, the heavyweight pillar of his imagination stood upright in a galactic night all its own without any of the consolations that lesser dreamers could comfort themselves with."

He went on: "To hear him speak of Auden, Yeats, Joyce, Kafka, Beckett, was to hear an equal, a Shelly plain, and the maturity of his comments swept away the champagne bubbles of romance that I sprayed on literature and revealed the steel soul of the cat I championed in all its mortal gravity."

Further:

He had committed himself by word and action to the league of the "immortals" and he was self-condemned to the isolation and only half-thereness that "immortality" demands of men and women who live in time. There was no childish competitiveness on the part of Klonsky vis-à-vis these stern figures, it was not to test himself in the ring of literature that he braved or broke the standards erected by these Twentieth-Century culture heroes (like my friend Mailer, who puts courage above reality) but rather it was because he had truly been born with a special line hooked into the inner switchboard of existence . . . in [an] extraordinary way [he] made abstract concepts real as your hand—like a religious Poe and

---

*The title comes from "Childhood" by the Welsh poet Henry Vaughan (seventeenth century): "I CANNOT reach it; and my striving eye / Dazzles at it as at eternity. / Were now that chronicle alive, / Those white designs which children drive, / And the thoughts of each harmless hour, / With their content too in my pow'r, / Quickly would I make my path ev'n, / And by mere playing go to heaven."

possessed a *spiritual* life so grave and proportionate that only the superbest adult utterance could do it justice.[17]

When I asked how it felt to be so lauded, Milton said, "Jesus didn't sue St. Matthew, but then he had *four* gospels."

In midsummer, with the birds singing and everything including myself relaxed (guard down), I lapsed into what I was to consider, for years, the most thoughtless, shameful thing I'd ever done—because of its unimagined effect on Milton. I had carelessly flirted by mail with a successful middle-aged author (in Milton's age group), never dreaming it might lead anywhere. The successful author came into town and surprised me by phoning. Thinking nothing of it, like walking a gangplank because it was straight ahead, I went to his hotel room. The taxi driver warned me that in such a situation things happen. But still, I was oblivious till the moment I realized what I'd walked into. When he made advances I felt so foolish, so absurdly naïve, that I spent the night. I did not think it would, at least, go any further. I thought the author himself would consider it a failure. However, he called the next day and I met some of his friends—Milton's friends, as it turned out. I brought up Milton admiringly. And that let the cat out of the bag.

Someone there reported to Milton, who phoned, enraged. He stormed over to Random House and I met him in the courtyard, quaking in my boots, also feeling the brunt of what I'd done. Driving the matter home, he said, and I will never forget, "I don't know whether you are like a child—unaware of the consequences of what you do. Or the most calculating person I have ever known." It was said in a fit of fury. But I felt I was both, which made me neither. I was mortified and overwhelmed with the realization that I had hurt Milton. I'd not even considered his feelings—thinking only of myself, that here I was in yet another situation where I led a male to have one expectation and my intentions were another.

A female friend, Nancy Wall, who soon afterwards was pushed

down an elevator shaft to her death in Turkey for misleading a date about her intentions, told me—just before her trip to Turkey—that she often ran into this problem; she could not make men understand when she did not want a situation to become intimate.

This was not Turkey and I was not in an elevator shaft. I wound up mortified rather than dead. I remained friends with the author, who knew nothing, I suppose, of all these feelings except that we did not want the relationship to continue. How could I have been so foolish, spineless? I didn't know except that I remember the flash of feeling: *"Not again.* I don't want to be again in this situation of saying *no.*" Of course, it was the most obvious time to say *no!* But my emotions did not know logic, frozen in typing myself as someone who unwittingly led a man on.

Nevertheless, Milton and I continued our nightly outings, and unknown to him, he continued to be the invincible, all-knowing Robert, desperate to secure the love of Patsy (later Paula) in my book.

There, I compared her meeting Robert to my encounter with the Mozart proxy at seven years old. I wrote that Mozart was "someone to catch up with, and so she became a writer at seven." Robert came as a reminder—"an old Mozart who didn't make it. He woke up competetiveness and ambition with the desperateness of a sleeper yanked out of bed to face the enemy. Again she was personally aware of time, and Robert could have been the back of the tennis court one hits practice balls against."

Yet to whatever degree this was a consideration, it never made it into the book.

I continued to collect his sayings. When he woke up with a cold, he said it was like finding a strange woman in your bed. "But I like to have a cold occasionally. It changes the weather of the psyche."

A friend of Milton's I admired was New Orleans–born author Anatole Broyard, a soon-to-be *New York Times* book critic. As if it were no secret, Milton immediately informed me that his latte-skinned friend with brown wavy hair (who'd served in the Army as white) had a "C" for colored on his birth certificate. Despite this open-secret status in the Village, Philip Roth, it was later believed, used Anatole as his model in *The Human Stain* (Roth's denial not withstanding).

At the Corner Bistro we might be joined by Broadway star/Oscar nominee Barbara Harris. Yet another friend of Milton's, whom I personally never met, was the poet Delmore Schwartz (later Saul Bellow's model for the manic-depressive genius Von Humboldt Fleisher in *Humboldt's Gift*). By the mid-'60s Schwartz lived in a fleabag hotel room paid for by "mad millionaire" Marshall Allen.

Sunday night, July 10, 1966, I got Milton to bring me in early. Too bad. Returning to the Lion's Head, Milton chanced upon him and they talked—shortly after which Delmore dropped dead in his own hotel lobby. Informed by Marshall Allen, a distraught Milton phoned me. He said that in their brief chat, "Delmore drifted in and out of lucidity the way people with brain damage do. But *sometimes he was totally lucid.*"

A couple of day afterward Milton evidently took it upon himself to claim the body in the morgue—doubtless at Marshall's request.

Recently, this discovery inspired the play *Klonsky and Schwartz.* By then, no one remembered about Marshall. Nor did the playwright seem to know that Milton had had a, as it were, magna-cum-laude array of friends.

The playwright hazarded a hypothetical relationship, presented as fact, assuming Milton was the person notified about the body. Of course, what the playwright did not know, and thus started the odyssey in the wrong direction, was that it was Marshall. The perverse assumptions continued to the point that Milton was assumed (in the play) to have been some sort of protégé, or underling, inspired by Delmore's death to charge forth and write books.

To support this argument, it was stated that after Delmore's death Milton did not talk about him, which (again) was far from fact. But Milton did not walk up to someone at a bar and tell a Delmore story or shout that he once asked Marilyn Monroe out (true). And was a close friend of James Agee, W. H. Auden (and so on).

Certainly he never blabbered that he believed Auden married *his* estranged wife to get close to *him* (he told me). *New Statesman* contributor Cyril Connolly noted (including Milton by name) that in every generation some writers influence those more famous but do not become so famous themselves—because, he speculated, they were "too proud to compete." This, Milton showed me with amusement.

Connolly wrote: "Our memories are card indexes consulted, and then put back in disorder by authorities whom we do not control."[18]

To be brutally blunt, it would be just plain character assassination to concoct a reemergence of Milton in the '60s based on menial protégéship to Delmore, in which his death provided a catapulting incentive (which the play—inventing most of the facts—hypothesized but was hogwash). I make a point to bring this up here because once a hypothetical gets presented as fact—if no one offers evidence to the contrary—it gets built on! And a whole house of cards is made out of fake biography.

I suddenly wonder if *this, right now, is what I was born to do—and the rest is training. March into the theater of life with a sword of facts left out that I can insert like jewels, changing the tenor, in some cases, the number of "levels of truth."* With levels of truth, it does not mean any level cancels out the others, by the way. That is why we are required, often, to expand, when our life is best interpreted by levels of truth we have not added in.

UNFORGETTABLE MEETINGS, 1965–1966—all in the same seventeen months, Legends in their own time: Jan Mensaert (Flemish poet, musician, artist), Milton Klonsky (New York City "poet genius," critic, editor), Hunter S. Thompson (the Gonzo reporter).

My Book on Unforgettable, Sensational, Flamboyant, Sensitive, Shocking Manifestation Models: the Men in My Life

**who influenced me and are now in the Spiritual Realms, some-
times affecting me from there too.**

Back to 1965–66, to the three men I met then, who set down
poles in my life on the strength of the meetings—which occurred
within the span of seventeen months. Beginning in 1966 the books
I copy edited sometimes made it to the front page of the *New York
Times Book Review* or became best sellers. Books of first novelists
included *Been Down So Long It Looks Like Up to Me*, the only book
by Dick Fariña, the Irish-Cuban writer/singer, husband to Mimi
Baez (sister of Joan), friend of Bob Dylan (see *Positively 4th Street:
The Lives and Times of Joan Baez, Bob Dylan, Mimi Baez Fariña,
and Richard Fariña*) and of Thomas Pynchon, who would dedicate
Gravity's Rainbow to him; Fariña died tragically on a motorcycle—
the back, not front—two days after the publication, April 30.

Recently, googling him, as I gazed at his photo he seemed right
there at my desk. Though initially bashed, *Been Down So Long* is now
a Penguin Classic. Pynchon wrote in the Introduction, "This book
comes on like the Hallelujah chorus, done by 200 kazoo players with
perfect pitch."

But what I did for that book was more on the order of allow-
ing erratic punctuation, with the proviso that the text be readable.
I'd studied grammar thoroughly, diagramming it on the blackboard.
As with Picasso (who could draw accurately, his father being an art
instructor), I thought it sometimes incumbent to break the rules—
adopt a different rule of creativity, where form reflects content. Thus,
if a situation was difficult, the language might bring the sensation of
effort. It might ask the reader to go through, in reading, the *sensation*
described. At least, I thought so.

About the time I worked on Fariña's book and *Papa Hemingway*
(A. E. Hotchner), I met Milton. I began to interact with Hunter
nine months afterwards. The three poles—Jan, Milton, Hunter—
were power figures, streetwise, artistic, authentic, outlaws, insisting

on it. I had no intention it be this way, but let me stretch my wings. I will scrupulously not walk on toes—especially my own, as I have a tendency to—and practice the closest allegiance to truth, to which I surrender and see where it leads.

— 5 —

On a Downslope

In Jean-Marie's sporadic letters things had progressed from bad to worst because unfortunately he was in Belgium. But he recounted the descent in tales barely credible. I have to say I did not consider him a "real person." He was "the Belgian poet."

In a museum retrospective I later described him: "like a fictitious character, someone that someone made up, who just 'fell out of the sky' (parachute and all). And managed to survive a fairly large number of years (more than he expected). He was like a fantasy character. But he was real. He disobeyed the laws of how to survive. But he was alive and real. He did not simply have a 'death wish' but rather an 'art' wish."[19]

He began enticingly: "Don't know how come but I feel in love with you this morning. Probably because the sun's out after seven days and seven nights of rain."

I read, sitting on the edge of my chair: "A couple of dramatic things happened, almost died of a heart attack. Had screaming parents and busy doctors all around. That's what I was told. Was too drunk to be aware of anything. Seems I emptied a full gin bottle, a couple of glasses of Pernod, a small bottle of whisky, plus wine and Irish coffee. The result is they hid all the remaining bottles."

Then, a friend "fell in love in a most desperate way and I'm feeling very embarrassed. Last Saturday night I was drunk again and she raped me." He pretended not to remember. "She suggested a divorce and eloping to Morocco. I told her that if she did, I would be sick of her after six months but feel obliged to stay with her because of the sacrifices she'd done and that we'd be perfectly unhappy ever after. Then she kissed me in a way she thought was burning with passion but was very much in the Portuguese-nun-kissing-the-Christ's-feet–style."

He was "running away to Paris in a couple of hours . . . The best
thing is to pretend I'm queer or impotent . . . Am dying to have you
back in Morocco."

In the following letter (December 1965) he'd returned to
Morocco:

> It's been a very long time now. Lost your address and
> had to wait for my parents to send it. . . . Am in a state
> which seems very close to insanity. Still the same problem,
> what to do with my life. Nothing very extraordinary. Have
> found the answer but don't know how to put it into prac-
> tice. Dream of spending my old days behind a window
> covered with frost, looking at the falling snow, far-away
> dogs barking in the woods, an open fire burning in my
> back, a pre-war German singer on the record-player. Not
> very realistic.
>
> Stopped drinking. Have hashish instead. Purposely. Am
> writing a new book. . . . Found a new house. In the Me-
> dina. It's quite something. Very old, very big and very high.
> Some sort of medieval dungeon. Splendid view and full of
> draughts, rain pouring in from everywhere. . . . Am living in
> the kitchen. It's the only room with an open fire.

He requested an immediate answer. "Wish you were around. I
don't think I'm in love. It's something else."

By February 16, 1966 he'd taken his "poetry to Belgium during
the Xmas holidays and the unexpected happened. My genius was
recognized immediately." He'd met an enthusiastic editor, who

> compares me to Baudelaire (which I don't think is very flat-
> tering as far as my strive for avant-garde goes), fell on his
> knees, thanking me for having picked him out . . . , is going
> to take care of the publishment [sic] and is convinced that

within a year's time I will be considered the most important Flemish poet and will deserve it. I see his point.

Apart from writing poetry I go on having daily has-chisch, the former being connected with the latter and that's all the news there is. Oh yes, finally resigned the contract. That was the first of February. I ought to be free the first of March. But probably won't. They won't let me. I actually hope they don't. The very day I mailed the letter I sud-denly realized I'm approaching happiness here as close as I can ever hope in this world, but for those damned kids and that's little compared to my Belgian nervous break-downs or my Siamese unsatisfaction. By the way, moved to a new place. . . .

I'm in a strange mood. An enthusiastic one for a change. You'll think me conceited but this time I do feel I'm writing good stuff. Don't judge from that November thing. Com-pletely different. At least, some is. Keeps me busy all day and night. I actually make poems while I sleep. Or dream I do. Which doesn't mean those verses are really good. I only feel it is. . . . But the feeling in itself makes it worth go-ing on. Probably a very common feeling and shared by the butcher who cuts his meat or the mason laying his bricks. But then I've never known what it means to work and this is work to me and it's a novelty as good as shooting rapids on the Me-Nam river in rotten sampans. To do something you like. I slave on it. There's the work at school, and aver-agely six hours of writing a day. . . .

I'm waiting for Moulay to bring my lunch. So will try to add something, Funny, there's plenty of things I want to tell and I always come back to the poems. I can't think of anything else. Even at school, while explaining I don't know what, I'm correcting what I wrote the night before or think-ing of something new. I don't dare to stop. I'm afraid that if I went to Tangier or Marrakech for a weekend everything would have gone the following Monday-morning. It almost happened while I was in Belgium. When I came back to Morocco my thoughts were blank. That was the hardest part. I obliged myself for two or three weeks to sit at my typewriter and to write down things I knew were humbug but it came back. Not little by little. One night it was there. Wrote 14 poems and if I hadn't been afraid that alcohol might have destroyed it, I would have treated myself with a big bottle of whisky to celebrate the homecoming. Take it easier now, but the fear is there very often.

I'm being impolite. I ought to ask you what your own writing is about but I can't. Do believe me, I am interested, I've often wondered why somebody who's got your taste, your intelligence and your culture (important too) spends her time correcting other people's prose, instead of producing, or, at least, combining both.

Wish you could feel the state I'm in. Don't run through the streets, shouting and screaming. But I'm feeling happy as I never felt before. Wish you could come to Morocco and see. It's so beautiful, too. Have [only] to turn my back to see miles and miles of lonely beach, a wild Ocean and huge clouds. It can't last.

My tagine has been brought upstairs. So, good-bye again. Send me your address. This time I will have it written on the walls of the house. . . .

Tell me if my brains are still good: home address 378 Bleecker str, NY 10014 Apt room nr 2.

This was *Poems from the Pawnshop*. Reviews labeled him a *poète maudit* ("accursed poet"): a poet who (explains *Wikipedia*) lives "outside or against society. Abuse of drugs and alcohol, insanity, crime, violence, and in general any societal sin, often resulting in an early death, are typical elements . . . The first poète maudit, and its prototype, was François Villon (1431–c. 1474) but the phrase wasn't coined until the beginning of the nineteenth century." Examples are Charles Baudelaire, Paul Verlaine, and Arthur Rimbaud.

I did not get my ideas from society yet was not overtly a rebel. At a distance this was a safe correspondence. I could read without judgment or personal threat from what disattracted me—of which there is much up ahead. I could maximize what felt genuine, slide over the rest, push it far down into the box, in that dream of the unending fall, the negative spiral, while the sparkle floated to the top. And yet a part of me could dare to write him any confession. The attempt to be interesting to such a person somehow drew out that part. How could he skirt so lightly around all the pitfalls he fell into, not sink to the bottom or even appear to have the need for processing and comforting? But skip from stone to stone of major episode to major episode, emotionally, lyrically described but not dwelled on after the fact?

Again, I could not understand it. It had the unreality of my character Ian. He seemed to dance on the rooftops of life, though with a distinct difference whether in Belgium (gloomy) or Morocco (productive). At the same time, being human, he was real. His accounts did not rise to the level where my conscience ran screaming to the offense, challenging the assertions. But some part of me rushed in to try her hand at *sounding* adventurous, searching far and wide for indications, hard to come by as they were. And any little "failure" could be recounted with no fear of rebuff.

My flamboyant side had found a match in Jean-Marie Mensaert. Knowing that in person he had a rather delicate appearance, I liked the fairyland he created, the never-neverlandness, the Peter Pan—the sheer artist genius and intellect behind it. I was fascinated by his pictorialness. I myself could not even draw. My tool was the pen.

Early on, Jean-Marie sent me a couple of his poems, translated. One, "Dance of the Sixth Veil," has Aziza imagine her death "just as the seagull dies somewhere unseen," or

as the dusk steps slowly across the evening
and without looking back at the sun which fights

with death and laments wails surrenders in red rattle,
without a sigh with dry eyes disappears into the night

Even more I admired his other poem, "*that I have met you makes me superstitious.*" It ends:

if children are more cruel than the ant on the worm
my heart is lighter than cork or foam on an atlantic wave
where seabirds can't float my heart sleeps
and nothing to bring doubt and everything is simple
for this is more than love
and you don't owe it neither do I

Meeting Hunter S. Thompson

You're a leprechaun. You come and go. You go off and answer some inner telephone, and then you come back till it rings again. . . . On the phone it seemed like you couldn't finish a subject. But you fill in the gaps with vibrations.
—Hunter Thompson

I met Hunter S. Thompson in 1966. It was a blazing mark in the sand, or sun, or sky—stamping the moment indelibly, that no removal of any sort could ever affect and nothing later ever put into the sidelight, or even shadow, in spite of all the shadow.

Hunter was twenty-eight. He'd written "The Motorcycle Gangs: Losers and Outsiders" for the May 17, '65 issue of the *Nation*—at the suggestion of its editor, Carey McWilliams. As part of the research, a *San Francisco Chronicle* police reporter, former Angel Birney Jarvis, introduced him to some of the gang. Hunter promised he'd tell their story honestly, then daringly began to invite them home to party. When the *Nation* story was published, the Oakland Angels president, Ralph "Sonny" Barger, liked it. Also, the very broke journalist suddenly received handfuls of offers to lengthen the article into a book.

Ian Ballantine, founder of Bantam Books and Ballantine Books, signed *Hell's Angel: The Strange and Terrible Saga of the Outlaw Motorcycle Gangs* as a paperback. Hunter chose Ballantine for the $6,000 guarantee, which included a rather puny $1,500 advance; it at least would pay the overdue bills. Only recently he'd been able to reconnect his phone, using the name "Sebastian Owl." Ballantine sold the hard cover rights to Random House.

The Angels rode low in the saddle on five-hundred-pound *chopped hogs*—seven-hundred-pound Harley 74s stripped of excess parts, the front extended, rebuilt for speed. Hunter rode a BSA Lightning 650. Wearing, he told a *Playboy* reporter, "levis and boots but always a little different from theirs; a tan leather jacket instead of a black one," he hung with the Oakland and Frisco chapters about a year.[20] The result was *Hell's Angels*.

As early as 1964 he had written friend Paul Semonin that he distrusted power and authority, and anyone who attained it "by conventional means—whether it is guns, votes, or outright bribery." That the two major present-day evils were Poverty and Governments. He'd considered beginning his *Nation* piece: "In a prosperous democracy that is also a society of winners and losers, any man without an equalizer or at least the illusion of one is by definition underprivileged."[21]

In September 1965—with "six months of massive [*Hells Angels*] research to distill" instead of plunging into his novel *The Rum Diary*—he wrote William J. Kennedy: "I feel like I've been hoisted toward the sun on the end of a very sharp sword, and the first wrong move will do me in for real."[22]

Hunter met Kennedy in 1960, when the latter, who'd studied creative writing under Saul Bellow, was managing editor of the English-language newspaper the *San Juan Star* (Puerto Rico). After an application to the *Star*, rejected by Kennedy, Hunter went to Puerto Rico for *El Sportivo*. A lifelong friendship ensued. In their all-night conversations the two avid readers roamed the canon of Western literature. Kennedy later won the Pulitzer Prize for *Ironweed* and became a professor at the University at Albany and at Cornell.

Prior to landing at Random House, Hunter explored South America as a reporter and sought every odd job imaginable in the United States, from selling blood to lining up with winos to deliver circulars. Already in 1965 he'd written: "Facts are lies when they're added up . . . you have to add up the facts in your own fuzzy way, and to hell with the hired swine who use adding machines."[23]

Another old friend, David Pierce, played a key role in the *Hell's Angels* publication *in stealth* and required everyone involved be sworn to secrecy. To this day no one has revealed it. Desperately tracking down Pierce in 2008, I located him en route to Thailand—about to disappear. Fortunately, for *Keep This Quiet* he withdrew the oath. Below is some background.

In the 1960s, Pierce, a good-looking, intelligent attorney, worked twelve hours a day and lived in a beautiful house with teak floors. In the heyday of hippies he was mayor of Richmond, in the Bay Area. He reminisces jovially.

"Here's a typical Hunter Thompson story. Hunter hung out at my house because there was a lot of drugs and booze and he was broke. He kept telling me I should go see the Hell's Angels. I had no desire to. I thought of them as being a bunch of really disgusting scamps. As usual, he had this sheepskin coat with this big tape recorder on his back. So I finally agreed and I put on an old dirty pair of Levis and an old shirt and we go to Oakland [to a] scumbag pool hall."

Within minutes Pierce left. Hunter followed. "And again, as usual, he has a bottle of Wild Turkey right beside him in his old beat-up car." To make a long story short, Pierce, who handily and overwhelmingly carried the African American vote, told him, "Tonight's celebrity night in Richmond. This black club on the South Side would really like me to show up *because I'm the mayor.*"

At the club, they "get completely smashed. They got transvestites dancing on the bar, the whole damn thing."

They left at two 2:00 a.m. Hunter was, as typically, parked right out front in the bus lane. Three policemen had the car surrounded. Though Pierce tried to make nice, Hunter liked the odds for a fight. Behind Hunter and Pierce was a sort of Greek chorus softly murmuring, "You're the mayor, asshole. What you kissing ass for? Those

fuckers work for your ass." One cop, overhearing them, conveyed the
news to the other two and charges were dropped. Insisting Hunter
was drunk, the officers made the loaded mayor drive home followed
by three cop cars.

Hunter had two large swords on his wall, and another time they
sword fought in the street: "So . . . we're *whacking* [said with the
sound of wind in his voice] the swords back and forth and of course
the neighbors call the cops." The cops asked for ID. Pierce showed
his. Hunter said his was in the house, come on in. Inside, one whole
wall was filled with unpaid traffic tickets! They instantly handcuffed
him and took him to jail, leaving Pierce to get him out.

Another time, around 1968, Hunter asked if he liked a certain Country Western music; Pierce said it was "rinky-dink." Hunter
took out a gun and shot him in the chest. The bullet was blank. But
the weapon was a .44 Magnum. "Now, a *blank* of a .44 Magnum will
knock you all the way across the room. I just thought I was stunned
and he was nuts." Hunter followed Pierce to his rented house, and
through the window Pierce saw him piling cardboard outside, setting
it on fire. He called the cops.

Pierce reflects, "So Hunter could be really sweet and everything. But he could also be extraordinarily painful and stressful to
be around."

At the time, Pierce continues, "I was on my way to India, to leave
and abandon ship, which also pissed him off because he thought I
ought to run for governor"—to make a difference. "I said, 'I don't
want to run for governor. I want to get outta here.'"

Pierce quit politics to follow the great Swami Muktananda. Joining the guru's inner circle, he organized his tours for four or five
years, then went to Saudia Arabia to seek a fortune selling fresh ice
cream on the road to Mecca.

I was twenty-six, having been one year at Random House—in what
was a fascinating job. With the guidance of the superb head of the

copy editing department, Bert Krantz, everyone got the best training possible. I have to say that Hunter was the most eccentric and flamboyant, even then.

Though largely unknown, he had admiration in house including from publisher Bennett Cerf. And certainly the trim, dark haired, middle-aged editor in chief of the Trade Division, Jim Silberman—who had visited him in San Francisco when Hunter was sitting on the manuscript. He'd been signed on the basis of the *Nation* piece, and as Jim put it, "With the first book, generically, you know you've got a good writer, you don't know if he can write a whole book. It's very complicated to get a whole book. He was having trouble—not writing. He was having trouble pulling the book together." So Jim "went out there to get [chapters] away from him." This was the beginning of a relationship that endured.

Jim and I worked well together. He found authors, did developmental editing. But it wasn't just business. He often said he "loved a good story." If I was his copy editor, we compared ideas in one-on-ones. Then he'd say, "Fix it up."

Ready with suggestions, I'd present them to the author in person, penciled in brackets in the text. Careful about sensibilities, I'd point out that a character's eyes were green on one page, blue on another. Or an age discrepancy. Or that a fact did not check out. I called the *Daily News* for harder-to-verify facts. That established, it was time for less obvious suggestions. Strictly for my own use, I listed on paper where words were repeated, say on pages 6, 15, 82, 250, 333. My brain logged a strong or unusual word when it reappeared, whether to good effect or weakening the place it appeared before. I knew never to change for the sake of changing. With no computers, we cut with scissors, Scotch-taped, and photocopied, then gave the manuscript to the printer, who penalized for messiness.

With Hunter's manuscript, fully backed by Jim, I thought I'd been restrained. However, I learned from the *Fear and Loathing Letters* 1 that "the Bal/Random combine" had made minor suggestions earlier that provoked in Hunter "soaking sweats."[24]

Anyway, with me no one had to defend territory. I couldn't have been more astonished when the first mighty salvo of a Hunter challenge arrived.

From 8/28 ('66), handwritten in red ink on gold/orange paper: He "[didn't] understand those 'corrected' pages you sent—but am appalled at some of the sentences inserted to 'clarify' my meaning—which they may or may not do, but I won't have that kind of writing in my book. I'd rather be obscure. Just received word of lost Esquire sale & am tempted to burn the whole goddamn manuscript. If not, I'll proceed with the various corrections." That said, he added, "but don't send anything else—I'm too simple-minded to grasp all that stuff_____H."

Thus began the Saga of Publication. But it happened to fall right before Labor Day, when trying to take book-jacket photos, he was ganged up on by Angels and stomped. Though I don't remember his explanation to me, I take as accurate his public statement that he'd seen an Angel beating his wife and dog at one side of him and objected. Bloodied, he wound up in the Santa Rosa Hospital emergency ward.

According to the Postscript he added to *Hell's Angels*, Tiny rescued him "before the others managed to fracture my skull or explode my groin . . . I owe him a huge favor for preventing one of the outlaws from crashing a huge rock down on my head. I could see the vicious swine trying to get at me with the stone held in a two-handed Godzilla grip above his head."

How Hunter communicated this to me, I don't remember. But in a unique arrangement Random House gave him blanket permission to bill *their* phone for calls to me at all hours. Long distance was expensive. Originating in California, the call came late. For one, Hunter estimated $160 (in 1966). Hunter lived in the moment, by his instincts. In his night-owl vigils he wrote—all night.

Humorously, he assumed I was a kindly middle-aged overworked lady who never got ruffled. He told me he appreciated the calmness. For several months he labored under this impression, which he formed himself and I did nothing to contradict.

In fact, I was in every way unlike his preconception. At ten years old Hunter delivered milk. He leapt from the van, sprang over hedges; would not take *no* for an overdue bill. And raced back *on a furious deadline*: to get to the open van door so rapidly the driver never had to stop. As a girl I loved movie star hopscotch and the slalom (water-skiing on one leg); crossing the wake, feet slapping the waves; then springing—with empty space underneath. And I loved to look under boards. Our common traits involved what Hunter called (from F. Scott Fitzgerald) "the high white sound," or note. But this was like a blind date *at a distance* or an early version of *You've Got Mail*, chaperoned by the all-consuming topic, His Book.

I do not know how that early letter was patched up (the final manuscript clearly shows markings from our *two* hands, as in the page 16–17 display in the booklet accompanying *The Tapes: The Life and Work of Dr. Hunter S. Thompson*). Anyway, "Sept 15," he wrote from home at 230 Grattan, San Francisco. (The tightly spaced dots are his, not omissions from the letter.)

Dear Margaret Ann—

It is now four hours and twenty minutes past the midnight deadline for my leaving this house, but I'm still here, sitting in a heap of boxes and debris....and working on this, my final effort on what now seems to be a doomed book.

Before I start rambling, here is a note on what is enclosed. 1) The Lynch report—which I want <u>returned</u> to me, repeat <u>returned to me</u>. 2) The Birney Jarvis article, which I also want <u>returned to me</u>. 3) All the information you need to get the goddamn police records verified.

As a side-note, I should warn you not to take any of the following personally. Despite my fecal opinion of Random House in general, I appreciate the efforts you've made to get the book in print. I still have the feeling that you and I are the only people who've read it [this was

not true, in fact], and it's nice to know I've made at least
one connection. So consider this your valid cushion, if I
seem too ugly.

            For one, you were conning* [Hunter's
footnote: *unwittingly, I presume] me today about that
verification bullshit, which I quickly found out is impossible. I recall hitting a stone wall when I first tried to get
at the Hell's Angels records, but when I talked to you
today I didn't remember why. The reason, of course, is that
police records are <u>unavailable</u> to anyone outside the legal
machinery—as well they should be—and I bitterly resent
the stupid, uninformed gall of your lawyers in attempting
to send me off on what any law student would recognize as
a wild goose chase. It may be that in New York any citizen
can go down to the courthouse and pay 25 cents for a photostat of any other citizen's police record, but I doubt it. In
California they tell you to fuck off, as I was told twice this
afternoon. (There are ways, of course, and I happen to have
one—no thanks to those waterbrained shitheads whom
Random House pays for legal advice.)

            Court records (for individual cases) are
a different matter, and <u>docket sheets</u> are a matter of public
record. Thus, any interested citizen can get a photostat of
specific charges, proceedings and dispositions [margin note:
"or depositions"] involving any other citizen....that is, he
can find out what happened in any given courtroom on any
given day, providing he pays the fee, which can easily run
up to $1000 for a full transcript of a two-week trial.

            In other words, I couldn't possibly have
got photostats of the various police records (for individual
Angels) that you requested—at least not through normal
channels. I would, however, have been able to get records
of specific charges and arrests—along with specific dispositions—if I'd had the time to drive all over California for

about two weeks and trade insults with various county clerks.

Needless to say, I don't. You people have been aware for more than a month that I plan to leave this week for Aspen. You are also aware that I *recently* sustained a severe beating that was nothing more or less than an attempt on my life. I feel entirely confident that any viewing of photos taken in the wake of this beating will confirm the dead serious nature of the risks involved in my roaming for a week or so through the heart of Hell's Angel turf, trying to verify their police records. Before you urge me to have another try at it, develop those goddamn photos from the Labor Day run and compare my face (as pictured) with some of the other author-portraits you have.

So, for the following and abovementioned reasons: 1) personal risk, 2) illegality of the attempt, 3) geographical impossibility, and 4) a spitting contempt for whatever mind that brewed the notion that I should be sent off on this hopeless chase....for these reasons and three or four more, I am turning over the whole burden of this verification question to my good friend and attorney, David Pierce of Richmond. (That sounds like a wild and vindictive statement, but it isn't....Pierce is the only person I know who can get photostats of individual police records without recourse to a subpoena.) To wit:

After talking to you today I immediately called Pierce and asked how I might go about getting the Angel police records. He called the Richmond chief of police (Pierce just finished a term as Mayor of Richmond) and was told I was out of luck. At almost the same moment I was getting identical intelligence from the Attorney General's office. The cops are not about to give out police records to anybody—and especially when they're likely to be for publication.

After lengthy dealing, however, we came up with two possibilities. Pierce is handling the [Pat] Brown [gubernatorial] campaign in Contra Costa county and is thus on good terms with the Attorney General's office. I am not; they view me as a dangerous freak, mainly because of the Nation article on the Angels. Anyway, Pierce can get photostats of Angel records, *with the firm understanding that we will never reveal the source, regardless of circumstances* [italics added].

The second possibility involved a visit by himself to O. J. Hawkins. The attorney general's office had informed Hunter that very day that while it routinely rejected requests for individual police records, in special cases if requested in person, Deputy Director of the California Department of Justice O. J. Hawkins made exceptions.

Hunter explained: "The catch is that I have to go to Sacramento and persuade Hawkins, who apparently roams the state like a hungry chickenhawk and is seldom in his office....and the only day I can get to Sacramento is next Wednesday, Sept 21ˢᵗ."*

If that didn't pan out, "The illegal part [Pierce will] do for nothing, as a favor to me, and the routine searching of docket sheets he'll do for whatever it costs him"—to hire out. If Pierce did it himself, it would be $350 a day.

Next he dropped the bombshell: Pierce will "be in New York the week of October 15 and I can have him stop for lunch or a talk." Like most of his friends, Pierce had "suffered through this book from the beginning and will do almost anything to get it done."

In any case, he was "leaving Pierce in charge of all my affairs until I get back from Aspen." Even his belongings would be in Pierce's cottage. Pierce would handle "all calls, threats and press queries . . . He is well armed and I've been giving him pistol instruction."

*In the case of tightly spaced dots (usually four) reprinted in most of Hunter's letters, these were in the original. Nothing has been omitted. However, where there are three spaced-out dots, as here, this is the standard ellipsis to indicate I omitted something.

So that should get us out of the hole inre verification. Pierce is far more capable of handling it than I am, and since you said you were going to pay for it anyway, we may as well have it done right . . . and after Silberman queered me out of that Esquire $1000 I'd be inclined to ask $500 a day, just to get even.

I realize that Silberman and his lawyers think I'm obligated to re-verify all the facts I've already verified to my own satisfaction....but I don't feel that way. I've written the book the way I want it written and anything I wasn't sure of I noted on the manuscript—like the Marx, St. Matthew quote. The rest will stand up, and if the bastards want to sue, let them. The only thing that worries me less than lawsuits is the threat of being arrested for saying I ate a few bennies. (For a parallel here, see [Ken] Kesey's "Sometimes a Great Notion" inre marijuana.) In any case, I can do without the help of your ignorant, old-womanish lawyers; I wouldn't go into traffic court with counsel who thinks you can get a man's police record for 25 cents and a smile. If I get in trouble on this book I won't ask for any help from your hired hand-wringers....and in the meantime I don't want them hovering over the manuscript. They've fucked it up enough; I have all the problems I need without dealing with inept lawyers.

That's about it for now. I'll deal with the non-legal correx on the galleys. As for the rape penalty, I checked it at length and want my figure (1 to 50) left as is. This is a very complicated thing, for reasons I don't feel like explaining but if anybody bitches, refer them to section 264 of the California Penal Code.

Sincerely,
HST
Hunter S. Thompson

In all probability the R. H. lawyers were unaware of Hunter's swollen face, broken rib, and blocked nasal passage. Having vividly envisaged the perils of hunting down photostats of the rap sheets, he offered a quick-witted solution with the publication down at the wire. As to *our* being strangers, that was not in the cards.

The fifteen-page Lynch report on California motorcycle gangs that Hunter enclosed read, he wrote in *Hell's Angels*, "like a plot synopsis of Mickey Spillane's worst dreams."[25] It was prepared by the California attorney general, Thomas C. Lynch, in response to lurid press coverage of two purported heinous gang rapes in Monterey County by the Angels—later determined to be consensual. Distributed to state agencies in March 1965, it depicted the bikers as long-haired, bearded, piratelike depraved wild men, a ring in one pierced ear, a winged death's-head on the back of their filthy sleeveless Levi jackets. Law enforcement should by all means curtail these vindictive criminals who, wearing swastikaed helmets, Iron Crosses on their chests, attacked at will. No place was safe, even a private home or small bar.

But Hunter revealed a gross bias: for instance, the report "stated that of 463 identified Hell's Angels, 151 had felony convictions. This is the kind of statistic that gives taxpayers faith in their law enforcement agencies . . . and it would have been doubly edifying if the 463 Hell's Angels had actually existed when the statistic was committed to print. Unfortunately, there were less than 100."[26]

While the Angels were indeed unlaw-abiding and dangerous, he called out *Time* and *Newsweek* for swallowing the story whole—*Time* in "a high-pitched chattering whine, with a list of phony statistics."[27]

At the end of the book is an epigraph: "ALL MY LIFE MY HEART HAS SOUGHT A THING I CANNOT NAME.—Remembered line from a long-forgotten poem."

Beneath that, his personal mystique originally concluded the book, until a Postscript on the stomping was appended.

His mystique involved his BSA Lightning: "four hundred pounds of chrome and deep red noise." Riding it on the Coast Highway in the wee hours, having crashed once, he had the intention to "stop pushing my luck on curves, always wear a helmet and try to keep within range of the nearest speed limit." He went out "like a werewolf, . . . for an honest run . . . a few long curves to clear my head." However, in moments he'd be at the beach—the empty road ahead.

"There was no helmet on those nights, no speed limit, and no cooling it down on the curves . . . [W]ith the throttle screwed on there is only the barest margin, and no room at all for mistakes. It has to be done right . . . and that's when the strange music starts, when you stretch your luck so far that fear becomes exhilaration and vibrates along your arms."

At one hundred, barely able to see, the tears vaporizing, "You watch the white line and try to lean with it."

He is describing "The Edge. . . . There is no honest way to explain it because the only people who really know where it is are the ones who have gone over." Those who remain alive "pushed their control as far as they felt they could handle it, and then pulled back, or slowed down, or did whatever they had to when it came time to choose between Now and Later."

The edge is "Out there. Or maybe it's In. The association of motorcycles with LSD is no accident of publicity. They are both a means to an end, to the place of definitions."

Another of many great insights in *Hells Angels* was on those who've "blown all [their] options." The Angels understood, Hunter wrote, that "very few of the toads in this world are Prince Charmings in disguise." Revealing his astute powers of analysis, he went on: "A toad who believes he got a raw deal before he even knew who was dealing will usually be sympathetic to the mean, vindictive ignorance that colors the Hell's Angels' view of humanity. There is not much mental distance between a feeling of having been screwed and the ethic of total retaliation, or at least the kind of random revenge that comes with outraging the public decency."[28]

From an Aspen P.O. Box October 5: "Quick answers to your letter that's across the snow-road in the main house and which I can't get now."

He'd sent Jim Silberman a proposed photo for the cover—his full-length naked backside, with a glimpse of a shotgun he was aiming. Alternately, he suggested a montage: naked backside, motorcycle shot, and the beating "mug shot"? He wanted the dedication to read: "To Ron Boise and Sandy Bull."

Boise was a sculptor, Bull a musician. I was to confirm Bull's death with Vanguard Records ("Could be bullshit, but I'd appreciate it if you'd check. I'm not sure how we can verify Boise's death, but probably Ginsberg would know. My sources are not always reputable, but they are not given to conscious lying").

Another Bay Area favorite of Hunter's was folk singer Rosalie Sorrels.

In 1964 the *National Observer* assigned Hunter to write "What Lured Hemingway to Ketchum?" He was to talk to Idaho locals who'd known Hemingway before his fatal gunshot wound at home in Ketchum in 1961; in fact, I myself (while working at Yellowstone Park) visited Hemingway's grave when flowers were still fresh.

So Hunter walked into a Ketchum bar, the Leadville Espresso House—converted from a bell-topped church in which Rosalie's grandfather used to preach. It was there that a grieving Kennedy family, mourning JFK, had a private New Year's party in 1964. The night Hunter walked in, he was to meet several lifelong friends: Milli Wiggins, whom he was to call "the Style Queen of Sun Valley," was there. Michael Solheim managed the bar. (Solheim later ran Hunter's Freak Power campaign.) Rosalie was singing.

Rosalie said, "Hunter was a sap for sentimental country music. I had Mitch Greenfield as a guitar player. I sang [Utah Phillips's] 'I Think of You' ('I think of you as the night rolls by. You're on my mind the whole night through. Far away in a lonesome city'). And he asked me to sing it again. I said no, I already sang it." He bribed her with a double shot—of *thirty-year-old* Irish whiskey. He kept buying her the expensive whiskey and she sang it six times that night.

Rosalie and Hunter hit it off instantly: "It was like meeting someone you'd known all your life."

Like him, she hadn't finished high school. But both devoured books. In her two-story log cabin in the Idaho mountains, she has five thousand. In conversation she could throw in offbeat quotations, which Hunter liked. Their politics was similar. They "had a similar imagination—[which is] how you think things ought to be and how you know they are.

"He had good taste in sappy romantic songs. . . . I thought [Hunter] was shy; he used to always put his hand in front of his face so you couldn't hear what he was saying."

When she lived in David Pierce's guest house in the Bay Area, with a cult following after her first album, *If I Could Be the Rain*, Hunter would take people, including critics, to see her at a Berkeley folk café. Once he brought Freewheelin' Frank, a Hells Angel, and it didn't get her fired. In fact, he was very polite. He told her, "Ma'am, you could sing the paint off the barn." Hunter wrote, "Some of Rosalie's songs are so close to the bone that I get nervous listening to them." Hunter's own version of their first meeting—from the liner notes he wrote for *Travelin' Lady*—went like this: "I think it was a night in California when I almost killed myself on a motorcycle . . . I was too full of pain to sleep, so she made me a pot of tea that was half Wild Turkey, as I recall, and then she sang for me until I finally passed out around dawn."

Rosalie told another story: Years later at Hunter's funeral she wore a fuchsia skirt and orange shirt (or vice-versa), and a man came up to say, "I'm Johnny Depp." She said, "I know." He said, "Yes, *but who are you??*" When she told him, he said, "Hunter loved your music."

By October 7—his return address still the P.O. Box in Aspen—Hunter had tracked me down at my parents' (on my birthday).

Gleefully, he writes, "I trust you understand the implications of questioning the seekout ability of a man who can locate the right Harrell—on the first call—in Greenville NC."

The idea that my research should require
verification is in itself absurd, but I suppose that's the way
you people do business. I trust, however, that it's RH money
that's being used to pay Pierce, and not a levy on my royalties—as in the case of Ginsberg's poem. If it were left up to
me I wouldn't pay a cent to get verifications; I'd rather take
my chances
in court.

Anyway, I've sent the necessary stuff
to Pierce, whom you'll be seeing sometime soon. I was
half-planning to zap off to NY with him, but the fact that
Esquire claims an IBM machine ate my check has pretty
well eroded my fiscal position for a while. The bank of
Aspen has agreed to pay all my checks, at $2 each, until the
Esquire check arrives to wipe out the overdraft. In the past
two days I've chalked up service charges (bounced checks)
totaling $14, and I expect about $10 more on Monday. For
this, and other very similar reasons, I don't think I'll be able
to make a quick trip to NY next week.

I told Pierce to get all the verification
material back to you by Nov 1, and I suspect he will. If it
necessitates any changes I'll dole out apologies all around
the board.

I'd playfully suggested he paste the galleys on the walls. He replied, "I don't own—or even rent—any walls these days." He didn't need "more useless work to confuse me. All I want is to get the goddamn book published and out of my head." He fantasized, "Maybe the Greenville paper has an opening for a good sports writer....or a crime reporter. I'm tired of this cannibal league." Signing "Sincerely," he printed: "*I am, however, concerned about the cover—art & copy—send material on this ASAP."

Letters intensified—as Pierce's trip to NYC neared. Oct. 12:

> I was a little disturbed yesterday when Pierce's investigator showed up here in Aspen. He wasn't aware of the rush on the verifications and seemed to want to do the job totally—to immerse himself, as it were, in the author's experience. I tried to impress him with the urgency of things and this morning he left for the Coast. But when you see Pierce you might warn him that his people are getting a trifle overzealous.
>
> As for other matters,.....to wit:
>
> 1) I still haven't sent the <u>About the Author</u> bullshit back to Marilan [Jim Silberman's secretary], but Jim says it will all be put into "jacket-ese" anyway, so I don't see where anything I write will make much difference. (Maybe tonight I'll re-do that first graph....if it's enclosed, you'll know I stayed up long and tragically.)
>
> 2) I want another name added to the dedication. Let it read this way: "To Ron Boise, Sandy Bull & Carey McWilliams....for various good reasons." Yeah, we'll have to drop that last "Sandy"....it changes the tone....
>
> That's about it for now. My infamy seems to have preceded me here and the local hoods can't seem to distinguish between writer and subject. I may have to take an ad in the Times to assure the populace that I'm not here to look for a fight.
>
> O. K. Tell Jim I want to be put on the mailing list for any and all publicity material regarding the book. I feel left out. My aged mother, who works at the library in Louisville, assures me that the book will be out

Nov 8, but I think she might be mistaken. I want to know these things. And don't give Pierce any grass; it scrambles his motor impulses. Sincerely—

HST

Hunter's book had been combed by lawyers, which was standard procedure. Except the concern went so far as to balk at his use of the term *Pepsi Generation*; in context, it might provoke a law suit by Pepsi!

Since August, Hunter and I had been conversing under the kindly middle-aged lady caveat—warriors together, late-night talkers oblivious to our appearance or past. Now his representative arrived with verified police records of charges never filed. Fortunately, Pierce has removed the restriction from revealing his role. I caught up with him in 2008 in, of all places, Durham, North Carolina, thirty minutes from my house (en route to Thailand indefinitely)! He took me to lunch. And we reminisced. Wearing a Panama hat, carrying a Thai bag, standing in the lobby of an office building he used to own, he was vividly alive. His skin still smooth, his face full, his body trim, his head covered with silvering hair, his smile contagious. Years removed from politics, he laughs at the tale but doesn't remember what files he brought. Rosalie Sorrels confided, "Pierce has a criminal mind."

Given advance notice about Pierce's arrival at Random House, I chose my clothes carefully, appropriate for walking up the long flight of stairs. Alerted when to expect him, I'd been told to lead the visitor up from the ground floor. I thought it would be funny to see how he reacted, watch his face as he made the discovery that I was not forty-four but twenty-six. It brought out my sense of comedy.

I remember distinctly, as if caught suspended in time, walking up those wide twenty-odd steps, marble-floored (to Jim's office). I was wearing a tight-fitting black and white wool plaid skirt and a black turtleneck sweater, stylishly tight. I led the way deliberately, conscious of the effect. It amused me to lift the lid on the secret of my age. I still remember the startlement between us, as if time halted as we made that climb step by step. I had dancer's legs, was twenty-six. I wore small heels. Every shocking contradiction to expectation registered.

Random House on Left

Pierce reported back to Hunter. Here the great Gonzo creator's sensitivity kicked in, his ability to be embarrassed—his ears and nose quickly detecting delicate emotional situations. Now he had to replay earlier scenes. Hunter could, on a dime, make the sleeping unconscious conscious. As he'd written in *Fear and Loathing Letters* 1, there was "what I call 'the psychology of imposition' . . . the need to amount to something"; that is, "If only for an instant, the image of the man is imposed on the chaotic mainstream of life and it remains there forever: order out of chaos, meaning out of meaninglessness."[29]

If physical attraction *might* play a role, every nuance counted. I'd known these details earlier, but there was something innocent about me by which I did not exactly look ahead and foresee consequences. There was no immediate reaction, no shift in the next letter. But in the Bay Area in November, he would see Pierce and sparks would fly.

Oct. 21: Hunter writes that his "new address, until further notice," is Owl Farm, Woody Creek, Colorado:

Dear Margaret—

My hands are so cold that it's hard to type, so I'll make this short. I'm glad to hear that Sandy Hill is alive and I hope he's doing well in his calling, whatever it happens to be. The second name in my dedication, however, is Sandy <u>Bull</u>, who blows (or blew) a guitar the same way Ron Boise blew metal sculpture. But if Sandy <u>Bull</u> turns out to be alive, strike his name and leave only one: <u>Boise's</u>. Also strike Carey McWilliams's name; he's alive too. This business of dedications is an awful thing . . . hell, let's strike Boise, too, and make the thing honest and have it read this way:

<u>To the friends who loaned me money and kept me mercifully unemployed. No writer can function without them. Again, thanks. HST</u>

OK, that's that. No names, dead or alive. I still want a page for a note on the lawyers, but I won't insist on the Spider poem ["Collect Telegram from a Mad Dog"] or the naked photo—although I still want to see the cover material, front and back, before it's too late to make changes. Enclosed is my corrected version of "About the Author." Pass it on to Jim and tell him I don't want it changed. Thanks—

Hunter's "Mad Dog" poem had been published in *Spider,* a radical U. C. Berkeley magazine, during the Free Speech Movement in 1965. In it Hunter's alter ego broke the face of a lawyer "with a running Cambodian chop." One line reads: "Norman Luboff should have his nuts ripped off with a plastic fork." In *Hell's Angels* the poem would have registered his objection to the restraints imposed on him to avoid lawsuits, such as having to change the names of some protagonists. The inclusion was vetoed by Random House.

Dated only "Saturday night," a letter zoomed onto my desk—from Sacramento. The "NV" postmark is barely readable now, but I believe it was mailed November 5. The outside return address says: "Luther Scarlett, 205 Crest, Oakland, Calif." Hunter was visiting Pierce in Richmond, hearing Pierce's tales of his visit to Random House.

Four strips of black tape seal the envelope. In erratic, dancing professionally printed letters a cartoon figure with owl-rimmed glasses and green shirt says—out of the corner of his lips—to a small astonished, attentive bird: "KEEP THIS QUIET."

Hunter's reaction below to Pierce's *live revelations*—and the phone call it precipitated—speaks for itself. In the 2008 interview, when I pushed Pierce as to what he told Hunter, he did not recall other than "You were very attractive." He thought a moment: "It must have been the legs.

"Let me tell you a related story: I'm in Manhattan. I'm staying with my friends the Gelbers. [Jack] Gelber wrote *The Connection* [1962]. He was a pretty well known director and playwright. I'm walking up maybe Ninety-second Street . . . towards the Broadway entrance to the Underground."

As he approached the subway Pierce suddenly noticed a beautiful young woman in front: "All I can see is the back of her legs. And the sun is bouncing off her legs and she looks really great. We go through adjacent turnstiles into the subway and have one second of eye contact. We get on the same car. She sits down on the same side, a few seats down. All I could see was her leg kicking up and down. She got off at Forty-second Street. She stood in front of me for a minute, dropped a note in my lap and got off the subway. And the note said, 'What would life be without fantasies?'"

<u>Sat nite</u>

Dear Margaret/

Very hazy now — just hung up. I think the bill for that call will be about $160. I hope you called quick + charged it to Random.

It's now six, your time — very wired up +

②

Listening to Sandy
Bull + the Jefferson
airplane. A wild
electric feeling on
every moment — and
all the other
freaks asleep.

   Nothing more to
add except maybe
an apology for
cutting off so abruptly.
It seemed necessary.
Part of my nervousness
was the sudden,
general electricity —

but that always
depends on what's
happening and
somewhere toward
the end of that
conversation I
realized that I was
looking for excuses
to keep you from
hanging up. which
is a bad state for
an impressionable hill-
billy to come to
Anyway, I felt the
panic coming on and

④

had to get off the
line. But I guess
I'll still come by
+ see you when I
get to NY. I'll be
a bit nervous, so
the talk will be
pretty difficult for
a while.

In the meantime,
bear down on the
book and remember
the SPACE.

HST

apologies for Pierce's
G. village envelope

Black-taped to a fifth page were two bulges (5 mg. Dexedrine pills): "sort of a temporary zapp. 4–5 hours duration. Not at all dangerous. One at a time—at least until I get there. H." I still have them.

By "remember the <u>SPACE,</u>" he meant not to let anyone shrink the inches and inches of nothingness that set off his epigraphs and newspaper-width quotes.

Another call from Hunter and Pierce followed. On "Nov 123" he hoped I got "that last phone call charged off to Random House when you hung up. One of the refugees sleeping near the phone that night told me it was even lengthier than I thought—some frightening amount of time":

> When you find out what it cost, let me know. I have a morbid curiosity about such things. But if anybody bitches, remind them that most of the calls Pierce and I thought we were charging to Random House were actually charged to that police precinct station (PL 6-1200), which was an honest mistake, but very fitting. It should make for some interesting activity in the police department.
>
> Did you try those pills? I'm curious about that, too. And I also remember that 10th st is not next to Bank, but Charles. The brownies again. I've decided to give them up.
>
> The drive back was wretched, 1200 miles of empty snow and mud, listening to election returns and getting drunker by the mile. A crisis at every gas station, due to my use of an expired credit card with a girl's name on it. I was lucky to avoid arrest. At least temporarily. My checks are bouncing all over town and I only go in at night, so I won't have to haggle with merchants and bankers. The bank thinks I'm still in California and will naturally take care of my overdraft the moment I return. Unfortunately, I have $8 to my name—so if you or anyone else there would like to be included in the dedication, by all means feel free to send as much cash as possible. I am

sounding a general call for funds to meet this emergency.

Otherwise, it's peaceful here. Deep in the Woody Creek canyon with hillbilly music on the radio and coyotes yelping somewhere out there in the night to keep the horses upset and the dogs barking. Every now and then I step outside and rap off a shot with the .44 to re-assert my authority. It stops the coyotes and echoes back the canyon like an atom bomb.

Not much else to report at the moment. It's 24 minutes before five and I need sleep, so I'll quit. Send word if any new problems arise, or call (303) 925-2250.

```
And charge it to PL 6-1200.

        Sincerely,

        THE WIZARD
           of
        Woody Creek
```

Hunter once lived in a 57 Perry Street basement, *very* near my current address on Bleecker between Charles and Perry. Also, he'd studied at Columbia University, my stomping grounds. Was that a slip of *the date*? "1-2-3" went a pop hit—"oh, that's how elementary it's gonna be . . . fallin' in love with you was easy for me."

Fortunately, the next letter is dated clearly: November 8. In his bid for sheriff later, part of his platform would be to curtail the "greedheads"—gobbling up property to build condominiums and hotels that further convert Aspen, the small Rocky Mountain ski town, into a jet set retreat:

Life is much calmer since I got word of
the Penguin sale, which should give me enough to at least
pay my debts, if not prosper. Incredible snow here, biggest
storm since 1934—two straight days of heavy snow. It's all
I can do to walk 50 yards from the main house down to my
writing cabin. The country snow-plow is a constant menace,
heaping up six-foot walls of ice and mud across the entrance
to my access road. Woody Creek is sane, but in Aspen there
are four-foot drifts in front of the bars and people with New
Jersey license plates skidding wildly across intersections,
scaring hell out of natives. The influx of ski bums is awful
to behold: they are an ugly, empty-headed lot, bumming
drinks on the street and stealing dogs and groceries out
of unlocked cars....most of them have seeped in from Los
Angeles and Chicago, a rancid and fitting tribute to mayors
Daley and Yorty. . . . If I lived in Aspen I would build a wall
in front of my house, but out here I don't have to....the road
up the canyon is an adequate barrier; for the first time in
about six months, I feel safe from both the Angels and
the Tong.

```
and that always means a deluge of bullshit.

wall in front of my house, but out here

canyon is an adequate barrier; for the first

fe from both the Angels and the Tong.

                              Sluggishly,
```

7

The Martyred Wizard in New York

Hunter was still being hounded in November. The lawyers were taking no chances. His book was going through scrutiny not given other books I had worked on. Not at this stage, anyway.

At this point Hunter was a stimulating author I'd been assigned to keep happy (by giving 100% to his book and answering his late-night calls). It was a thrilling unorthodox job situation with strong professional demands, except that there were moments which inescapably slipped in, in which our emotions signaled they were on high alert because of the feelings this contact brought.

November 14 he pointed out the gross unfairness of the lawyers:

> Here's some of the stuff you asked about. I couldn't find the UPI clip from Dallas, but as I recall it was sometime in August of 1965. I recall reading it to Bill Murray ([Saturday Evening] Post) & he was in & out of my apt that month.

The reporter Bill Murray was, of course, not the actor Bill Murray, sixteen years old at the time.

> Anyway, I've gone through two huge boxes of material looking for it and I don't intend to do any more looking. If you or anyone else had mentioned it back when I had all my material separated into chapters, I'd have had no trouble finding it. But now all the stuff is lumped together and it's only a matter of luck that I happen to have it here at all. I'm not in the business of verifying things I

already know and if anybody had warned me that I was
going to be plagued endlessly with this kind of bullshit I'd
have written a different kind of book. Next time I'll dash off
a careless first draft, getting the writing over with as quickly
as possible, and then sit back and wait a few months until
somebody gets around to reading the fucking manuscript
and gets me going on the really important business—six
months of haggling over meaningless minutae [*sic*] that
couldn't mean a goddam thing to anybody but lawyers.

Why in hell didn't somebody mention
these things to me when I first sent the ms. in, when I was
still on top of things and could have checked everything in
the course of my normal work? You wait until I get 1200
miles away from the scene and then ask me about things I
have no conceivable reason to either remember or file. And
I have to do all this goddamn work for nothing, putting off
other work that I could get paid for. I'm completely out of
money, with nobody around here to borrow from, so far as
I'm concerned I've finished with this bullshit. I've done my
work. I not only wrote the book, but researched it about as
well as any human could, and my agent sold part of it to
Esquire while you people muttered about the New Yorker.
And on top of everything else I got stomped trying to get a
cover photo. Fuck it. I'm finished. It's your turn now.

Other items: the Whitright letter is
enclosed. See the first and last paragraphs for what may or
may not amount to permission. I think it does, especially
since I called her . . . and specifically asked if it was OK to
reprint the letter. She said yes, and since nobody mentioned
written permission until six months later, I had no reason to
think there was any more work to be done on that angle. . . .*

---

*The widely spaced dots on this page indicate I omitted something from the text.

Also enclosed is the Jerry Cohen article,
but the Wall St. Journal Xerox machine left off the date.
It appeared within a week or so of the Angels' 1965 (July
4) run to Bass Lake. No earlier than the 5th, nor later than
the 15th. My guess is July 10-11-12. I didn't bother to read
it to see if I used Cohen's quotes in the order he published
them—but since I was standing right there during the
entire interview I don't see that it matters. Throughout
the book I tried to mention other reporters and writers by
name, because it seemed like the right thing to do, but so
far it's caused me nothing but grief. I was under the impression that I was writing the story as it happened and as I saw
it, but you people have made that almost impossible.

Also enclosed is the Chronicle clip with
the misspelled name, Ken Craik. At least this (the Craik
spelling) is the way the AG's office had it. You can take your
pick—on this and all the other material Pierce got from the
AG. I don't have much faith in their information, but since
you're more concerned with photostats than with truth, I
suppose you'd be better off sticking with Lynch and his half-
literate, desk-bound boondogglers. . . .

As for the [Sonny] Barger telegram
[from the Oakland Angels founder], I enclose a clipping
and copies of both the telegram and his statement that was
handed out at the press conference. It's all a matter of public
record and I can't believe we don't have the right to use it
without payment. However, since you insist on making
work for all of us, go ahead and offer him $25. I should
have told you [on the phone] today to send him a check for
$25 with the stipulation that he return the signed release
at once or we'd paraphrase the signed release and he'd get
nothing. If he has time to think about it he'll call a lawyer
and there'll be no end of mad haggling. I tried Pierce twice
tonight and he wasn't at home. . . .

Into the envelope he dropped a Hell's Angels–Oakland dance ticket, Nr. 161. Donation $1.25. Beer 25 cents. I taped it onto my mirror. It said on the reverse side: "To Margaret / with best wishes for a bopping good time."

In another early appearance of his alter ego—in this case, "The Martyred Wizard of Woody Creek," which is how he signed the letter below—on November 23, he admits, "Your phrase 'absentee landlords of the spirit' pretty well describes the way I feel about the New York end of my literary activities."

He had not received the *Esquire* galleys for an "Orgy with the Angels" excerpt and predicts: "All manner of legal hell is likely to erupt over that one. . . . They took what they wanted out of my uncorrected carbon, and I have no idea what they're using." He recollects no orgies: "But I guess it depends on how you look at it. Anyway, don't mention this until the issue is on the stands. Let the bastards get burned. Maybe next time they'll have the decency to send me galleys."

Battling insolvency ("The Woody Creek store gives me everything I need on the cuff"), he concludes: "I still can't breathe through my nose without the constant aid of prescription nose-drops, which are brutally expensive and a bitch to carry around all the time. Remember to send all those clippings, etc., back to me when you've finished with them. And let me know when you need the set of galleys I have."

```
nd all those clippings, etc. back to
with them.  And let me know when you
I have.
                    Sincerely,

                       THE MARTYRED WIZARD
                         of Woody Creek
```

After I paid Sonny Barger the $25.00, I got patted on the back. My letter to Barger, Hunter said, was "Tough, quick, etc.—no

surprise that he signed. Pierce hustled him & is now being threatened because the $25 isn't paid—please handle this. Pierce is wor-
ried. They know where to find him."

Often at night I'd stroll into the Village with Milton Klonsky after
correcting R. H. manuscripts in his apartment while he read thick
books. Milton prepared meals—rare steak rubbed with garlic, pep-
peroncini as a side. And we ate on cushions at his low coffee table.

Millionaire Hy Sobiloff had hired Milton to teach him to write
poetry. Sobiloff's sister dated Marlon Brando, who would land in
a small plane on the Sobiloff yacht. When Milton escorted me to
Sobiloff's Thanksgiving dinner, which was served by butlers, the provocative actress Shelley Winters yelled across the room as we left,
"The next person I'm going to sleep with is Milton Klonsky."

Milton said that night—in response to *what* I don't know—"I *too*
have a pilgrim soul." (This was a variation on Yeats, about his mostly
platonic love of Maud Gonne: "How many loved your moments of
glad grace, / And loved your beauty with love false or true. But one
man loved the pilgrim soul in you.")

As much as I tried for a Maud Gonne–type relationship, he
pushed it toward the physical with all the trimmings. And he did not
give up easily. Often he quoted Andrew Marvell, "If we had worlds
enough and time this coyness, dear, would be no crime." On January
6, concerned that I might have misunderstood after taking me to the
filming set of the *Kama Sutra*, Milton telegrammed: GIRDLE OF O,
GIRDER OF I. INVIOLABLE. UNBREAKABLE.

"I" and "O" were "Io" ("I" in Dante).

I'd dated Milton over a year in a very profound relationship. Not
(on my part) sharply romantic, though with an undeniably high volt-
age. Regarding amorous physicality, thanks to me, it was stuck.

Eventually *Hell's Angels* went to press. Writing December 16,
Hunter asked me to convince the publicity market not to target the

book to "the Argosy–Popular Mechanix market." He'd shot an elk:
"—big meat for the winter." And was shopping for "a hill-climbing
bike."

He finished: "Impress on Silberman (and Selma [in charge of his
publicity]) that I insist on coming to NY—& if Random won't pay
for it I'm coming anyway, and I'll be in a goddamn ugly mood if I
have to pay my own way. See you then/H."

On the reverse: he was thawing a huge buck in his writing cabin—
"getting it nice & ripe so I can put it in Pierce's bed [at Christmas] &
blow his mind—the head & skin are still on—and big horns, too—
very gruesome—like a frozen corpse."

In December, I received the newly published *Gedichten uit de
Berg van Lening* (*Poems from the Pawnshop*) by Jan Mensaert. It was
strange to receive the first book by "the Belgian poet" the same month
Hunter's was at press. I was looking forward to Hunter's arrival in
New York.

By then I was hard at work on *Other People's Money* by playwright/
novelist Jerome Weidman (*I Can Get It for You Wholesale*). Weidman
graciously autographed *The Sound of Bow Bells* December 25, "For
Margaret Harrell, who would have made this a better book . . . all my
thanks comma and not a little awe." I remember coming upon him
talking with Bennett Cerf as I left my office with another author—
that author starstruck at the sight.

Just after New Year, Hunter wrote. He added his new red-and-white logo:

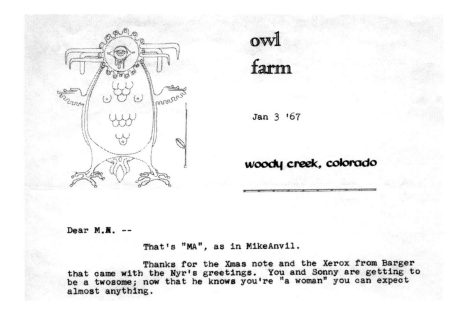

owl
farm

Jan 3 '67

woody creek, colorado

Dear M.N. --

        That's "MA", as in MikeAnvil.

        Thanks for the Xmas note and the Xerox from Barger that came with the Nyr's greetings. You and Sonny are getting to be a twosome; now that he knows you're "a woman" you can expect almost anything.

Anyway, you neglected to send a copy of his previous letter in which he described "Hunter's beating." Send it at once. I am not concerned with his accuracy, since he wasn't there, but his general attitude and stance will give me a good idea what to expect when I go over to SF for publication. Interpreting a letter from Sonny is like an exercise in Krimlinology; you have to know what every word means in the Angel context. Probably I can tell from his letter what sort of armament I'll need when I go back to SF—and also what sort of publicity gigs I should risk [in the book tour]. As I said before, I have no intention of being stomped again, even if it means getting jacked up for manslaughter. So far I've heard two versions of the stomping: one, that I deliberately started a fight, and another that it was all a tragic misunderstanding. Both of those are bullshit, and I'd like to see Sonny's version because that's the one that will be the official line.

As for here, Snow, Snow, Snow, Snow, Snow....brutal cold, frozen pipes, sheetice roads, broken cars, the whole winter gig, Rocky Mountain style....I'm trying to work on the novel but it's not working and I spend most of my time writing vicious letters. Did you ever take those pills? [No.] Merry Xmas—HST

Before arriving in New York, Hunter sabotaged the trip. First he suggested, in a letter, I "get a huge raise if this thing makes any money. Not many people would have tolerated all of my bullshit during the check-out era, and I'm sure you worked harder on the manuscript than anyone else - - - - - except me, heh. Anyway, I'll see you sometime around the 15th."

Then the bummer: Repeating that he was "cultivating a bad case of nerves," he said he'd need "plenty of strong drink on hand at all times." He'd be in a "terrible, nervous, drunken, freaked-out condition so try to be polite."

Finally, Jan 30, handwritten in red: "Dear M. A./ Very peculiar call today—I think you're going mad."

In this final letter prior to his trip he ordered that we not import actor Jack Thibeau or Pierce, etc: "Don't make any arrangements to have me accompanied by a rooting section . . . I'll have a hard enough time keeping straight without a bunch of heads following me around. If you're interested in getting Pierce to NY, for christ's sake don't schedule him while I'm there. Put him on TV after I've gone—he can deal with the lawsuits. That's what lawyers are for." Furthermore, went the chilling expectation: "I've already made arrangements to have McGarr—an Irish advertising geek—meet me at the airport on Feb. 14. We will then begin drinking heavily, in preparation for my Feb 15 performance on 'Today.' If Selma [Shapiro, who handled his publicity] has any ideas about keeping me sober for TV, she'd better be ready to stay up all night."

He declared himself "perfectly capable of lining up my own accompaniment—from native stock." He warned, "If anybody from west of the Hudson tries to tell Selma that they're coming to NY to 'help me out,' tell them to fuck off. OK for now. HST."

We'd been thrust together at a monumental time. What's more, told to go through this together, it was paid for and required. What would happen when we actually met?

I woke up on the morning of the fourteenth (or fifteenth?) with butterflies. Hunter would be at Random House that afternoon. Jim had promised he'd bring him by my office.

The thing was, neither Hunter nor I had ever seen the other. I had the advantage of a photograph. He had only the description of Pierce, who could have been putting him on, and more than that, beauty is in the eye of the beholder. Anyway, perhaps he wouldn't show. I had almost fallen for Pierce but restrained myself, and Hunter was somehow aware of that.

In the last letter he'd written: "If you're interested in getting Pierce to NY, for christ's sake don't schedule him while I'm there."

Pierce had all the qualities and appeal—fast talking in an interesting way, beautiful to look at with dark hair and expressive eyes, very very intelligent. I had restrained myself, on the off chance that a bird in hand was not better than one in the bush and that Hunter would be even better than Pierce in person. But who knew? And perhaps he wouldn't find me interesting in person.

Perhaps he wouldn't go the mile to take me out, being married to someone else. I thought he and his wife had mutually consented to see other people, which was far from the truth, I found out later. Anyway, would I want to go out with someone in almost every way inaccessible—including distance.

For whatever reason, I had discarded those obstacles. Truth be told, I didn't think it through. I felt the strong pull that both of us had acknowledged as the electricity went over the phone wires in pauses and we couldn't touch but the vibes did it for us. We had stayed mostly on the subject of the book, as the letters show. But the book was him in a way. His first. He had all his energy invested in it, and that was a lot, and I was part of the deal.

In the afternoon I was waiting in my office. I looked at the climbing leaves and did some work on a manuscript. But I was waiting for Hunter Thompson. He would be in the building today. I hoped he would come down to my desk. There was no assurance of even that, except that how could he not? Our attraction was pretty much unspoken but equally obvious. However, he'd sabotaged this meeting in his last letter, hurling out an attack as if daring me to withstand it.

So I was waiting, sure the business relationship was strong and so was the romantic feeling, which was impossible to push aside. I didn't want to. I didn't think he did or could.

To enter the office, there was only a door frame. No door. Suddenly a face peered round the empty frame: Jim Silberman. With an amused expression he said, "I have someone I want to introduce you to." That was it. Hunter stepped in. A giant, six feet four or five, beautifully built, with sandy blond hair and brown eyes. His cheeks dimpled. He didn't speak or reach out to shake my hand. We were beyond that stage, even though it had never been voiced. What he did next would captivate me—by his ability to magically dispel my bountiful self-consciousness. His, too. In one hand was a brown shaving kit. He reached down as Jim's and my eyes watched but particularly mine. Instead of making conversation, he was caught up in this act of unzipping it.

Need I say more. I didn't care what was inside. We were totally focused on this shaving bag and his hands—as they pulled the zipper open and I had no idea what to expect. Perhaps it was a variation on what was to happen later that night. Perhaps that's what relaxed me. I don't know. I just know that every shred of self-consciousness in both of us vanished. We were like two people on the same note of music. And what was inside the bag?

Two Ballantine Ales. He took them out and offered them up: one for him, one for me.

Thus ended the first moment of seeing each other, which is always a test. How will a fantasy hold up in reality? How will the vibes, the physical sensuality of a person, the telltale signals of attraction hold up, the depth that was definitely there be able to carry the weight of the dark eyes and dimpling mouth that was acquiescent, not wildly speaking and gesticulating. As he raised his eyes from the shaving kit it was all over. Our eyes met and he asked me to wait backstage while he appeared on *To Tell the Truth*.

He thought I would help him not be nervous. Hooray. Hooray.

He wanted me behind the scenes, to know I was there.

In those days, when there was basically one TV show at a time, practically every station in the land carried *To Tell the Truth*. In that game three contenders pretended to be the mystery guest. To detect bluffing, a celebrity panel quizzed them before voting. Finally, the moderator pronounced, "Will the *real* Hunter S. Thompson please stand up?"

With self-revealing amusement, the cutest, most boyish-looking, unassuming guy raised his head; then bent it downward. Sporting short sleeves and a sleeveless jacket, he flashed a modest-looking grin. Watching backstage as he rose out of his seat, not overplaying his hand, dazzled me beyond all description.

Who *was* he? There was no indication how complicated that answer was.

The way he captured that moment, the unexpected surprise that broke the suspense as he rose from his seat, revealed the presence, the shenanigans—the unpreviously authored script—of a genuine self.

The dashing six-foot-one Irish advertising geek, Eugene McGarr, joined us. Gene and Hunter had been copyboys together at *Time,* and Hunter had once had a mailing address, c/o McGarr, 245 West 104th Street. They are known for such escapades as the Leroy Street Massacre and the Gregory Corso Massacre.[30] McGarr would become one of the most successful voice-over artists in the country. His trademark was a handlebar mustache.

After dinner in the Village we all went to my apartment to listen to the music we'd bought in the afternoon: the two Jefferson Airplane albums (one of Hunter's favorite bands but new to me) and also some Dylan, LPs that made Hunter's heart sing. And mine as well.

The San Francisco sound was psychedelic. I loved it. The sound and the leaps in imagination. And even though not lighting up a joint like Hunter, had no trouble at all falling into the mood. Against the bare walls of my second-floor walkup, the Airplane's "And I Like It" roared—and whispered: "This is my life, I'm satisfied. So watch it, babe. Don't try to keep me tied."

It would become our theme song. The music was loosening me up even more. Music does that to me. But I didn't need loosening up by that time. We were just in sync. Conversation was sparkling. Then another top buddy, William Kennedy, came in and Gene left. And the pot cigarette was passed around. I would pass it. I don't know whether I puffed it superficially or just passed it, which was also acceptable. In any case, I was not smoking. I was drinking gin and tonics. Not excessively but socially.

At the very end of the evening it was obvious Hunter was going to stay. I was deeply smitten. You might say swooning. But to actually sleep with him if he was not in a good condition would throw away this incredibly long buildup. It should take place in the right circumstances. I didn't feel like a manic spur of the moment thing or one-night stand. I had to convince myself what I already knew, that it was more than that for him. So I was very relieved he wanted to stay but asked him to sleep on a single mattress on the floor beside my bed.

He thought this was odd. "I feel like a dirty old man," he said. But did it.

So he was sprawled out, his long frame covering the floor mattress beside my primitive single bed. And of course it was too tempting. Once he'd yielded, my point was proved. I felt valued if he would "wait for me." And that ended the wait. I laughed and told him to get into the bed. We completed the passionate attraction that nothing would stop, then and there.

Hunter has often written that he preferred the "high white note" of Scott Fitzgerald to sustained continuity. The split second, or evening, of reaching the top of the mountain. That forever-alive memory of something one did even maybe once in a lifetime. We would not have sustained continuity. Rare and far apart would be the times we could meet. But the meetings would be unforgettable. That night we started the tradition of snatched moments.

It was the beginning of a physically passionate affair that would last several years. Though the meetings were few and far between in tight clusters, it was one of the most profound relationships of my life.

Kennedy said, "The pleasantest visual memory I have of that night is you crossing your legs and revealing a bit of garter and stocking top, tan stockings. Cheered me up. Lucky Hunter is what I thought."[31] He added, "I thought you would have become a theater actress or movie star. I left and Hunter stayed."

8

Hunter: Rendezvous in L. A.

Some things Kennedy remembers better than I. The book launching was the first time he saw Hunter "in costume." For the tour Hunter wore bizarre sunglasses and a cowboy hat, his first. "I'd never seen him dressed like that. Ever. . . . He was presenting this new persona. It was the *costume element* of his outrageousness. He hadn't bothered with the costume focus before; he was just outrageous. . . . He was putting on a show for this public event."

The next day I reminded Hunter that he had threatened me just before his arrival, writing "Dear M. A., I think you're going mad." I asked him why he'd laid it on thick.

He didn't even remember that but speculated he'd been *pouring cold water on a fire*. He said it would be *like* him to write something alarming, in this instance. I was startled by the honesty, the self-awareness. He even admitted it immediately. I was greatly drawn to such an open-book approach. I wasn't used to the style of mea culpa, stripping away all guilt. This wiped the slate clean, preempted a hangup or the blame game. I adored such a unity of reality and feelings. In a geography as complex as the narrow streets of an old village he made the maneuvers straightforward, no matter how convoluted underneath. Again, he had taken me inside the game plan. I adored it. Had he not fessed up but been sneaky, all enchantment would have evaporated. I was, in my own writing, using the image of someone who "if you pushed and shoved did not crumble."

He asked: "Do you write anything yourself? I've almost never met anyone who feeds on words the way you do. Like a cow. You chew on them, swallow, bring them back up. . . . You're a leprechaun.

. . . You go off and answer some inner telephone, and then you come back till it rings again."

He can see right through me, I thought.

He continued with a winning frankness: On the phone "I thought you were giddy . . . couldn't finish a subject. But you fill in the gaps with vibrations."

I thought: "Perfect characterization. *He* talks with vibrations."

I know these words were just as I wrote them because I jotted them down on a piece of paper I still have.

The next few days the Airplane and Dylan pumped up the volume, sealing the attraction. Prophetically, "And I Like It" filled the apartment, promising, as if reading the future, "This is my way. . . . *my-y* dream. . . . I need mo-ore. . . . 'ore, 'ore, 'cause this is my-y time. . . . So watch it, babe. Ain't gonna be like the rest."

No, I knew he wasn't *gonna be like the rest.* "So why not git away from the mess. . . . Ye-eah, this is *my-y* life. You know I like it . . . You know it's *mine.*" I kept singing one line in my head, unrealistic and not thought through, but there it was. It would linger through the years: "Why not fit your life in with mine?"

The impression afloat afterwards was that in his press appearances Hunter was exhausted, drunk, or a no show. The official line, as told by Paul Krassner (in "Blowing Deadlines with Hunter Thompson," *One Hand Jerking: Reports from an Investigative Satirist*), was that during the tour Hunter had been "either a blathering drunk or an insane mumbler" (reprinted from his email to me December 27, '06).

"I don't know why he mumbled," Kennedy said of one show.

But my live notes portrayed it differently. I took them to help jostle his recall for a press-tour exposé that Krassner engaged him to write for his satirical, infamous West Coast magazine the *Realist*.

Asked on the *Today* show "Are they homosexuals?" Hunter wrestled aloud: "*How latent is latent?*" Finally, he deflected: "To me, the whole question is irrelevant."

In a jam with a caller he searched, then: "Christ, it's Bishop Peale."

Elsewhere, not in my notes, he hilariously squirmed out of a tight spot with "Help! Help! Help!" (Years later it might be: "Goddam, man. Who wrote these questions for you?" If not "Hee-haw.")

In thanking a *New York Times* book reviewer, he mentioned "strange plastic freaks babbling at me, asking stupid questions, no hope of human communication."[32]

In my exposé notes I took the issue to be irrelevancy. I wrote: "What you really needed was a lawyer to stand up and say, 'Incompetent, irrelevant, and immaterial.'"

In 1958, Hunter had written about the philosopher Spengler's distinction between people of action and of thought. Hunter named it a "psychology of imposition."

He debated whether *he* imposed himself on reality through action, *then* wrote, or imposed himself *by* writing. Or both. In the 1967 press appearances he did not necessarily impose his viewpoint except by implying it. You had to follow his mind working, which I found easy.

The irreverent Krassner, a stand-up comic, journalist, and social critic, later inducted into the international Counterculture Hall of Fame, had met Hunter the preceding year while emceeing a Vietnam Day Teach-In at Berkeley.

Hunter arranged to meet Paul in the Village at a bar-restaurant. We sat, and the table exploded with brilliant, fast conversation. I remember only a few things: the sense of a dark room, Paul across from Hunter and me. Paul talking about how he loved to feel life on his skin, feel the rain on his back, the snow—uncovered, unprotected. He spoke with intensity. Fortunately I scribbled down a few comments afterwards, so I know they are word for word from that evening:

Hunter objected, "Every time I go away from the table something happens."

Paul quipped, "You slow down our conversation."

Hunter: "I don't like leaping around without finishing a subject. That's mauled conversation."

Paul also said: "One thing about arguing with Hunter, he refuses to defend any point a minute after he made it."

I wish I'd recorded more. I believe it was Paul—it sounds like Paul—who that evening quipped: "Hunter, you always want the apocalypse."

Yes, indeed.

He autographed a book for my mother: *Dear Mrs Harrell/ Thanks very much for your offer to pay my San Francisco phone bill, but the probation office has made other arrangements. Sincerely, Sr. Bobo.* "Bobo" was one of his many nicknames for high school friend and author Paul Semonin—to whom he would write, "Dear Bigwind," "Dear Doctor Strangelove," "Dear Tail-Chaser," and sometimes "Well, Bobo." In *Hell's Angels* there was also a "Preetam Bobo," who might have been *San Francisco Chronicle* police reporter and former Angel Birney Jarvis.

A penciled/ink-written FYI note between Jim Silberman and myself is two lines: Me: "He's turning into a gentleman." / "Margaret—Extraordinary, Jim."

That week whirled by—every nook and cranny of my dreams fulfilled. With time short, we made the most of late evenings in my apartment. There, just before flying out, Hunter wanted a souvenir photograph of me. I'd shown him the three head shots taken by the professional photographer who stopped me in the street. I had them packed away in a drawer, but he easily drew me out. There was one copy of three different shots, as if of two entirely different me's. The serious shot ended at the top of a turtleneck sweater, my neck engulfed in rolls of wool; he liked it and said: "It's just short of being fake, though it's not fake."

A bare-shouldered head-and-neck pinuplike shot, he liked but passed over. He chose a combination—of the two me's. As he took that home he muttered, with no explanation, "Wait till Sandy [his wife] sees this."

Extremely let down after he left, my energy plummeting, I doubled my vitamin dose, which did not pull me out of it. Making an uncharacteristic doctor's visit, I was prescribed medication. It didn't help too much that I received the following letter, which opened vistas of Hunter finding out about the slipup I'd made shortly before meeting him, about which, regarding Milton, I was remorseful to the point of thinking it the most awful thing I'd ever done—because I'd unwittingly gone right into the circle of Milton's own age who had "made it," while he refused to turn commercial. But it shows how the truth can be a stalker, forcing itself out.

I have only page two of this letter, dated February 24, from Gerry Feigen, MD, chairman of the board of *Ramparts*. I had phoned Feigen on behalf of Hunter; *Ramparts* was running a favorable *Hell's Angels* review. But he wrote back personally.

Page two begins: "Life forces defy serendipity; there are numberless crossroads which are never touched by intersection. Alors! I was out in the Manhattan chess game, ears to the quick, alert, urgent talkers, feet on the trembling floor, eyes on the stars when you called. I sensed a mote of paradox [that he was at the pad of Random House President, Robert L. Bernstein]."

That wasn't the troubling part. He'd told [the author with whom I'd had the indiscretion] that he "got imagery by phone, and . . . a voice that fit the essence. I suspect that you will not lose in the original. I used you to spin a gossamer, seamless web at 39,000 feet coming home. Not knowing has its advantages for fantasy. . . . . shy, shapely, Southern? Maybe laugh and cry poetically? Landing didn't erase it all. Life lines can't be camouflaged."

I was trapped like a butterfly in my own thoughtless web. I admired Feigen's poetical turns of phrase. But was mortified lest he now pass on such tales to Hunter!!! Fortunately, either this did not occur or Hunter overlooked it, never making the slightest allusion to it.

Finally, Friday evening, the phone rang. Well, it was about time. It was Hunter—in L. A. on press tour! He right away attacked the literary quality of Dick Fariña's *Been Down So Long It Looks Like Up to Me* (I'd given him my signed copy). *He'd thrown it against the wall!* he said. I listened. Surely this wild rant was not the reason he'd called. Surely that was not what was on his mind. Then he murmured—difficult to hear—that he wished I were there. Understated. But enough to pick up on. You had to be attentive, not let those all-important words slip past. Not say: *What? What was that he just said?* Not be too bashful. *"I can be,"* I hurled out.

I hurriedly washed my hair. Normally for special occasions I had my hair done. Hunter said he'd repay my ticket eventually, when he got some cash. I had a low salary for New York except that we received a bonanza—when R. H. was required by the government to back pay unpaid overtime. To pay for the ticket, I probably did what I often did in those days—signed my father's name to a check (my own name underneath), which was perfectly legal in those days.

I remember, etched in memory, wearing a white cotton wraparound miniskirt (my first). Miniskirts were new (to me, anyway). I hooked my nylons with a garterbelt, taking pains to keep the seamed line in back straight.

In the LAX mirror I appraised myself beside Hunter. What I saw filled me with horror, freezing the moment in time. I will never forget. Reflected in the mirror, the skirt rode up with each step, at which cue the garter belt hooks peeped out! The rest not bad: deep-lavender satiny T-shirt: sort of hugged the breasts—not too tight—draped well; dancer's legs, long red hair falling over one eye. True to form, at no point did Hunter utter one word about the garter gaffe!

Meanwhile, the Random House publicist, Selma Shapiro, phoned. Told he was *en route to the airport to pick someone up,* she muttered it could only be one person. How did she know? Was it obvious I'd do something like this? he would welcome, encourage, participate in it, invite??

Now to luxuriate in stolen moments. I remember sitting at the bar, waiting for the taxi, proud and pleased that he had come to pick me up. Before the madhouse of press appearances we could take a deep breath and really pinch ourselves that we were in L.A. together.

Hunter was staying right on the Sunset Strip—in the Continental Hyatt (later dubbed "The Riot House"). Near the Whiskey a Go-Go. A legendary favorite of the Doors, Little Richard, Led Zeppelin, and the Stones. There were press appearances and in the evening a party, from which we retreated early. It gratified me that we hid out that night. And the next day ordered a luxurious breakfast in the room.

My impression of Hunter's eating habits was not that he was "the messiest, most piggish, food lout."[33] Also in '67 Hunter was not overtly using drugs in front of me, except sometimes pot.

I typically savored food and sometimes ordered three desserts, to take one bite of each. My breakfast, rolled elegantly into the room, centered around a to-drool-for cheese omelet.

To manufacture time in the afternoon, we did a disappearing act. The thing was, I had to leave early Monday.

Our expressions must have looked like the cat swallowing the canary as, slipping away, we rented a—what else?—convertible, smiling broadly while Hunter charged it to Random House, and whipped off, wind blowing through the open top, me wishing for a scarf, to the nearby—"Santa Monica, Margaret," I hear; "Now, liven this thing up!"—beach. The Pacific surf pounded to the left just beyond my view of Hunter's hairy arms; hilly sandbanks rose up on the right. Traffic was low. He had a beer in his hand. He drove with absolute alertness. Otherwise, I'd have objected. I would *never get behind the wheel after even one drink!* But Hunter's agility, his dexterity, were in evidence.

Here was a man who would famously pass a sobriety test when he demonstrated the split-second, coordinated reflex of, as his hat accidentally fell off his head, catching it in the air behind his back with one hand.

That was instinct, and he trusted his instinct. He'd tested it earlier when, having avoided LSD (even though it was legal till late 1966), he finally tried it. He'd been warned off it by the experience of a psychologist and/or by Mike Murphy, a cofounder of Esalen Institute, where Hunter was caretaker in 1961. It was impressed upon him that acid made some people—predictably himself—violent.[34]

But by the mid-1960s, Hunter gave in.* He likened the experience to getting down "to the bottom of the well."[35] Down there was no rabid wild animal.

Instead, his *instincts* were trustworthy. He would say in *Songs of the Doomed* that with acid, "[Y]ou can't pull back. . . . You can't repress anything. . . . If you're going to get violent, you're going to get violent. But I didn't. Instead, I usually get very calm."[36] He was not afraid of violence and perhaps for this reason did not bring up repressed anger and violence.

I like to quote from *Songs of the Doomed*, which Hunter gave me the last moment I saw him, in his chair in his living room in 1991. But we're not there, of course. We're in 1967, in a top-down rented convertible. Exhilarated—liberated—in the fact of stealing away, meaning no harm to anyone, carving out this nook where no one would ever know we'd been. Sometimes life allows that, something not drenched with consequences for drenched with sunlight, with permissions, with no retributions, with the warning to make the most of it, for it won't last, circumstances being what they are, so the heart is to open and it did.

I had no doubt this relationship had staying power. I'd no idea what he did away from me and didn't ask. I counted on something in him that carried around this tie.

Hunter said he liked to carry around special things in his pocket, figuratively speaking. So on that shore, we stole even more snatched bits of time to put in our pockets and draw out later in total trust that this excursion, the report of it, would never fall into the wrong hands. And it never did. Not even into the wrong heart. I believe that these two hearts remained firm.

---

* The Great Shark Hunt, 103, locates this first experience at The Fillmore Auditorium in San Francisco. In *Songs of the Doomed*, 114, as in the *Playboy* interview of 1974, he recalls having first taken it at Ken Kesey's in La Honda, south of San Francisco. In any case, in the mid-'60s.

But what kind of Hunter is this? No drugs. Let me tell it my way. Hang on. I would like to put on record that I never saw him DRUNK, that is, reeling, or even *in any sense* off balance—though on good authority he's reported to have been. I will get to all that later.

When we made our entrance again, Hunter explained—straight-faced with an ambiguous expression—that he'd had to "go out to change my shirt." Of course, he changed the shirt *because* we went out.

At midnight, no less, he was scheduled for a talk show radio appearance but walked off the set in a confrontation over not being given permission to sit alcohol on the table in front of him.

In the wee dawn hours—fulfilled, gloomy, feeling all emotions—I boarded American Airlines 294: seat 20A, final destination LGA.

On the blank side of the airlines folder, marked "For notes and expenses," I left now-cryptic penciled glimpses that—peered at for every drop of memory—turn the pages of time backward: "Many things would be better if they happened at a different time" (Hunter said) and "$71 meal in room"!!!

"Many things would be better"—yes, obviously. I'd been advised early on, by someone who knew Hunter, that he had an open marriage. I believed it, though I have since learned (much later) that it was untrue, in fact gossip. Yet I don't think knowing the untruth of the statement would have affected me. All I knew was that I would not refuse to have this experience. Of all the experiences I'd refused to have, this was not one. As long as I didn't think about the marriage, didn't imagine it in a real way, this "relationship in a void," which was its own little world, was ratified to exist there for as long as it did.

I arrived at work at noon Monday, no questions asked. I slipped behind my desk as if nothing had happened, telling no one. And work went on without a glitch. In my absence that morning Swedish copy editor Barbara Willson had received a letter from Paul Krassner. He had written it to her, *thinking that was me.*

Investigative satirist Krassner, whom talk show host Don Imus labeled a comic genius, is variously described on his website—called by the *New York Times:* "an expert in ferreting out hypocrisy and absurdism." According to the site, FBI files show that when *Life* described him favorably, the FBI wrote the editor: "'To classify Krassner as a social rebel is far too cute. He's a nut, a raving, unconfined nut." And Groucho Marx said, "I predict that in time Paul Krassner will wind up as the only live Lenny Bruce."

Krassner began the letter "3/2/67" under an exotic *Realist* letterhead: "Dear Barbara, If you ever decide to try LSD, this is just to offer my services as guide."

He goes on: "Incidentally—no, not incidentally—you are one of the most delicious females I've ever seen, and since there was already a mild establishment of intellectual rapport, I feel compelled to state my—to de-ulteriorize—my motivation." He "would like to make funny, passionate, friendly, cosmic, absurd love with you. Ho hum. I think I'll attach a questionnaire with this. It is not a form letter, by the way. Paul (Paul Krassner)."

Barbara—check one:

( ) I like your honesty. Please call me at _____.
( ) I believe in equal rights. I'll call you at GR 7–3490
                                        CA 8–6622
( ) Your honesty is appealing but I have a spontaneity hangup.
( ) But didn't you know I'm a virgin, and intend to
      remain one?
( ) I'm not a hymen-fetishist, but you're just not my type.
( ) You're my type, but I'm just not socially available.
( ) I'm a lesbian; do you have a cute sister?
( ) You men are all alike, you're only after one thing,
      blab bla bla. . . .

( ) I'm sorry, I can't go out with a man who doesn't drink.

( ) You'll have to get a new trench coat first.

( ) Ha ha, I'm not even going to send this back to you.

( ) I'm an independent spirit and I'm afraid you'll
     be possessive.

( ) I don't <u>have</u> to give you <u>any</u> reason, see.

( ) Barbara Willson is somebody <u>else</u>; you and I never
     even met.

( ) You writers will do anything to get your book
     published. . . .

Unknown to him, this one was half right: "( ) Barbara Willson is somebody <u>else</u>; and you and I never even met." Barbara turned the letter over immediately—downstairs to the Random House obscenity files. I wasn't told. Sometime later Paul phoned me at work. He said he'd asked Hunter's permission to invite me out. Hunter said yes. I winced. So Paul wrote the letter. Then told Hunter he'd invited Barbara Willson on a date. Hunter said fine, but who's Barbara Willson? Krassner was phoning to tell me to retrieve the letter, I'd get a kick out of it.

I retrieved it. Obviously, I would not say yes and wondered why Hunter would, but it was part of his contradictory character. Would he really not mind? Would he say he didn't mind as a test? Then I passed. So much blood shot to my head that I did not reason out the possibility that Hunter too had no idea what Paul was talking about.

9

HST: The Red Ink Letters

With Hunter back in Woody Creek after more book touring, trouble was brewing—at his instigation—with the Scott Meredith Literary Agency. Rather than Hunter's lawyer, John G. Clancy, writing the agency directly, I acted as intermediary, sending documents to Clancy at Pillsbury, Madison, & Sutro in San Francisco. Clancy wrote back, asking for a clear *page three* of Hunter's contract and a copy of the Random House contract form, to see what on *page one* Article 1(a) (iii) had been crossed out. Robert Devaney, Hunter's agent at Scott Meredith, sent the requested photocopy of the page "which was illegible in the original copy I sent you." I have a note penciled by myself: "iii License publicatn of a reprint ed by ano pub[lish]er w/ the consent of the Aut. The Aut. shall be deemed to have given consent if w/ in (20) days aft the forwarding of written request he fails to notify the pub[lish]er in writing of his refusal to consent."

By March 14 Hunter writes:

Dear Margaret—

       I just sent Silberman what might be a terminal letter. And a copy of same to [Bernard] Shir-Cliff [Ballantine Books]. Let me know if you quit or move to another publishing house. If I go first—and if you want— I'll insist that you be hired as my copy editor before I sign a contract. With a raise, which is more than you'll get from Silberman.

In the meantime, the enclosed package contains an Aspen leaf [silver bracelet], which you can wear, hide or sell, according to your instincts. [I wore it.]

I also owe you some money, which I don't have any of right now....but which might be available if Random House pays my "extra expenses" and also gets the $500 the CBC owes me. As of now, the only money I made on that tour was $5 from CBS, for signing a release. (And, excuse me, Krassner's $200.) Anyway, I'm just as broke as I was before I left here, and—with all the bookstores I know of unable to get the book—I don't see much hope of getting much money from royalties. I might, however, get something from a magazine sale or two. . . . The L. A.–Toronto–Aspen leg of the trip was an unqualified nightmare. There are a lot of other things to explain, too. Maybe I'll call.

Anyway, I'm here, and not much changed. Just tired.

H

Four days later he is "disappointed in [me]. In addition to doing Silberman's work, you're also becoming his apologist."* He rebukes me for defending the "same kind of cheap bullshit [that he] wouldn't accept from Time, Newsweek and the NY Times. I won two out of three—& really 3 out of 3—on that score, and those issues were

---

*Hunter had referred admiringly to Max Perkins, the one-of-a-kind editor of Fitzgerald, Wolfe, and Hemingway, when in contrast regarding *Hell's Angels*, "They made fewer changes in my 480-pg. manuscript than [Clifford] Ridley [the *National Observer*] normally made in a 10-page article" (*Fear and Loathing Letters* 1: 569). Hunter didn't then know about the system, whereby the next stage passed to me. Many senior editors specialized in contracting books, sometimes conceiving the idea, plus sweeping developmental editing (this was Jim). A few, such as Joe Fox, with whom I also worked a lot, edited line by line. Jim left the line-by-line to me. However, we had one-on-one discussions in perfect agreement; I remember how every time I left Jim's office I felt something decisive had happened—been settled.

far more open to interpretation than my argument with Random House." It was "un-nerving to hear you mouthing the corporate bullshit . . . after all we went through on the book revisions. I didn't work all that time to destroy a structure of lies, only to become a victim of it myself. As far as I'm concerned, R. H. is now just as fair game as Time & Newsweek."

It particularly riled him up to have been told not to look back. He ends, "I'll see you when the dust settles. Inevitably—H." Naturally, I didn't think Random House would be unfair financially. Jim, who was particularly decent, ethical, loved Hunter's work. He apparently had no problem riding out a rocky moment. It was the "golden age" of publishing, as he would fondly say, a time when "it was the book that counted."

Seeing nothing but humility and generosity from Jim, who once surprised me with an amazing Christmas bonus (I believe it was several hundred dollars), I thought Hunter was living up to his reputation of being difficult, though I knew nothing about the financial details. True, however, he was dependent on his writing for survival.

Replying, I pictured him with a "precarious bank account, everything on dubious credit, a Sebastian Dangerfield kind of experience where [Hunter] walks in, opens accounts in stores, and has no money to back them up—but not carried to quite that extreme. (The alternative: 'A hollow purse,' said Melville, 'makes the poet stink.')"

Dangerfield was the antihero in *The Ginger Man*, one of Hunter's favorite books.

By March 23, exploring changing agents to Lynn Nesbit, Hunter asked me to mail back his manuscript *The Rum Diary*. I'd made photocopies for him. Lynn had told him he was "screwed worse than I thought—yeah, even worse than that—so I'd feel better if I had all existing copies of the RD here. The game is going to get very ugly pretty soon. Thanks. Hunter."

March 27: He thanks me for having cleaned and mailed back his suede vest: "Much puzzlement & anticipation when package arrived. Only God sends things that big & unwieldy. How much was it?

I owe you quite a bit. Let me start with paying that cleaning bill.
OK‐‐‐‐‐‐‐”

I had been upset by his rebuke March 18. He put the fault at his doorstep:

> Forget my mean letter. You took it
> almost too seriously It was more of a root-anger, spur-
> of-the-moment thing. I've come to the point where any
> mention of Random House makes me foam at the mouth—
> and you just caught a wild punch. All your explanations
> were unnecessary—I know—so don't worry about it. You
> may catch a few more, but that's only because I can't get
> at Silberman & I feel a desperation to make some kind of
> contact with the Vicious Entity. It's only frustration and a
> need to shake somebody that makes me zap at you. But it's
> not aimed that way—"It's all right, Ma, I'm only dyin'" [the
> Dylan song "It's Alright, Ma (I'm Only Bleeding)"].
> As for your "Totally Disorganized
> Irrelevancies & Digressions"—well, I don't want to use
> any stupid clichés to say how they affected me, and I'd
> be embarrassed to use my own words—so I feel a bit
> inadequate.

What I recorded in the Irrelevancies & Digressions, I'd witnessed
on his book tour, on stage and off, and considered out of kilter with
his views. I thought he could get his teeth into my reporter's log. I
had also quoted from Dylan's "Ballad of a Thin Man." He went on:

> Feeling a contact is one thing, but seeing
> it in print is different. Despite what I say about the cheap-
> ness of words, I have a powerful faith in them—because
> maybe like Gut's bike, they're all I have. Or maybe not—
> we have to preserve the image. Let's say they're the only
> tangible thing I have—my equalizer, as it were, and I like

it - - - - (heh). And so much for that—the stealing of lines. Anyway, you did some fine notes. I'm not sure if this is only my ego talking, or something else. But I didn't get the impression you were aiming at my ego—more of a contact, by saying the right things, or maybe even the wrong things that were important.

I think I'll use the Dylan "dump truck" quote [from "Buick 6"] to lead off the Realist article . . .

He was outraged at lack of returns on his blockbuster book:

I've spent most of tonight working out the financial end of these dealings, & the final figures are absolutely bizarre. To wit: The 2 publishers' profit—including my $6000 advance and an alleged $19,000 for ads & promotion—is $297,750.00 That's at <u>wholesale</u>, or <u>cost</u>. (60% on hard cover & 75% on soft.) Salaries, rent & printing costs aren't included, but could they possibly be—on one book—more than, say, $97,750? Probably less than half of that.

And what's the maximum I can get—over a period of 2–3 years? $20,438—or 5% of the gross. That's not counting the two years spent writing & grappling with the book. Or 5 years at $4,000 per—obviously a bad hype—& that's why I said send the novel back [*The Rum Diary*]. It's not going to happen again. . . .

Whoops—I see that my 5% HST profit doesn't jibe easily with my other figures - - - (time to think & figure again - - - yeah, it does, but the whole thing is too much to explain - - - - later). So much for that. . . .

And that's why I yelled at you. I'd no sooner exempted you—in a letter to Silberman—from the vicious pawnshop ethic that he represents, than you turned around & tried to defend it. The fact is that you don't know, & it's better that you don't, so try to keep out of the money arrangements until you know the whole score. You are working for a bunch of soul-fuckers, and nothing Silberman says will change that reality. It's Time magazine by any other name—you just happen to be a strange human accident in the machinery.

And that's that, for now. Like I said, I think we're heading for an ugly period and I doubt we'll work on another book unless you change jobs. But don't take any of my railing & bitching personally—and don't disappear without letting me know where I can find you. And by all means let me know if you go to work for another publisher. It would have a definite effect on my dealings.

Jesus—what a depressing letter. I didn't mean it to be that way. This goddamn contract business has screwed up my mind—it blocks out everything else. . . .

Maybe it will be a good summer, but the prospects are ominous. I expect to spend a good part of it in court, trying to get the chains off my neck.

Christ, here I go again. . . . I wish I'd never heard the name Random House, but since that's already bad history, I'm glad you were part of it. Maybe we can do better next time. H

Rumor has it that during his press tour Hunter walked off the set of NBC's *Today* show. I think I can clear that up.

In a note April 1 to Hugh Downs (host of the *Today* show and former announcer for Jack Parr), Hunter thanked him for his help on the *Kup Show* and then *Today*. Kup's was, Hunter said, his first TV appearance. And when the famous reporter/columnist began with an overly general question, "'Tell me, Hunter, what do you *think* about the Hell's Angels?' I figured the best thing I could do was walk off the set. So it was a hell of a relief to have you re-phrase the question in manageable terms."[37] Later, in *The Great Shark Hunt*, he recalls disrupting the show in that appearance "by calling Adlai Stevenson a professional liar," whereas the other guests were there publicizing a Stevenson memorial.[38]

But the *Kup Show* was broadcast out of Chicago. Did Hunter touch down there en route to New York? I can't remember. To find out, I read Kupcinet's autobiography, *A Man, An Era, A City*—of his interviews and friendships with every celebrity from JFK to Sinatra to Harry Truman to Dietrich. But there was no mention of Hunter— even when Kupcinet listed the guests who were silent or walked off the set.

By April 5, his ruthless persistence had produced some success:

Hello—

I'm here again, with a moment of peace. And maybe an apology. I say "maybe" because I'm not sure what Silberman and Shir-Cliff have done....if I believe what my bank says, I'm overdrawn, evicted, naked of credit and into the third day of waiting for Shir-Cliff's check that he said would be here on Monday. If it doesn't come tomorrow I'm going to take action—very loud action.

But that's neither here nor there. I have a very tentative new view of Silberman and since I'm admitting that, I'm also admitting that I gave you too hard a time in recent letters. But you also have to realize—and I half suspected you did—that I was talking to Silberman, to some extent through you. This is very hard to explain; I guess I'm admitting that I have some politician in me, and that in one way or another I used you to gain my own ends. [This sheer honesty went straight to my heart, the sense of presence of "the real person," even the soul in person.] But that's pretty harsh. A better way to say it is that I couldn't afford to forget that Margaret Ann Harrell, human being, was also M. A. H., Random House copy editor—and sporadic confidante of one James Silberman, with whom I had no way of communicating. And with whom I had to communicate, at least in some small way, or give up entirely on Random House. So in that sense, I guess I used you, but I don't see anything evil in it. And there's also another way to see it: that no reasonable person, engaged in a vicious power struggle, could be expected to gamble several years of his life and income on somebody he knows more by instinct than reality. But that's unfair too, because I knew that instinct was right even before I saw you....anyway, I gave you a harder time than I should have, and I'm sorry it happened. I didn't expect you to get so upset, or to assume I was misinterpreting those things you sent. They all worked...(three dots)...but at the same time I had to separate every human consideration from the contract argument . . . It was absolutely imperative to force the contract talk into a human realm...because in purely legal terms I was screwed to the wall. So I figured What the Hell? Screw it On and see what happens. Torpedoes be damned...and in every legal sense there were many torpedoes.

And fuck this. We'll talk about it sometime and I'll say it better. I'm obviously over my head trying to explain it in print. The nut of it is that I was Looking Back very hard, and I was angry on a level that you've never seen or dealt with. That's not an easy thing to explain when it's past.

The thing about your sending the RD back was phoney [*sic*], and it very nearly cost me that copy of the MS. It arrived today in shreds and tatters. As a matter of fact, the other two copies were torn up, too, when they arrived. There must be special MS envelopes for this sort of thing. Send me one and I'll return the RD.

The point of all this—and my last letter, too—is that I want to make sure you understand why all that bullshit transpired, and that I said a lot of things that were either stupid or angry or wild, or even calculated, but they didn't have much to do with you. I was talking essentially to Random House, and neither of us can escape the fact that you work for them.

OK for now. I have to get back to the Realist piece, then go out to SF tomorrow or the next day for some work on an article for the NYTimes magazine. And then back to finish an Aspen piece for Harpers and find a new home in my spare time. And a new car. And the Weimaraner is about to drop a dozen puppies on me.... and I can't leave for SF until the overdue Ballantine check arrives, and mainly I'm tired, tired, tired. If I get any material evidence that Silberman did what he claims to have done [he did], maybe I can rest in peace. Until then I'll be walking on my fangs. So until the dust settles, I remain, half-savagely, H

I had critiqued a story by Hunter's journalist pal Lee Berry. On April 15, I marched in a Vietnam peace rally of an estimated 400,000 people from Central Park in New York City to the UN building to protest the war, with Lee. Lugging a heavy typewriter, Berry then worked his way across the Atlantic on a Norwegian cargo ship. He sent me a postcard that began: "Hunter, Margaret."

Lee was trying to get a piece in *Cycle Magazine.* He said the war had created "much anti-US vibrations . . . They don't take it out on individuals but <u>do</u> want answers." Declaring little to report ("I am not Sebastian Dangerfield"), he instructed, "Margaret, please forward. . . . Tell [Jack] Thibeau."

I wrote Hunter: "Lee has appointed me Keeper of the Mails because he thought you would have a new address. So here's the first offering."

As he had virtually disappeared, I asked had he "gotten eaten by coyotes, or sucked into a marsh or down under piles of stories. . . . I got two postcards from Europe today—spring comes, and everybody's off. It's awfully tempting. Ye Olde Courier."

On May 29, '67, in red ink on legal paper he replied: "I know you're back there, doing most of Silberman's work—and I've been meaning to write for as long as I can remember. My whole world has altered since I got back—Sandy has become a total invalid, Clancy arrived at the far end of a nervous breakdown, & Semonin just got here tonight with his woman. I was also evicted & am now in the new house—still in Woody Creek & with the same phone #.

"Christ, I picked up the phone to call you & then decided against it—not much to say except that chaos still prevails. I'll call sometime soon at work, to trace various manuscripts."

He intended to complete the Krassner story and predicted that by end of the summer I'd be "wrestling with the RD, . . . loud, vulgar & treacherous." He'd bought a new bike on credit—"so if all goes according to plan, the RD will be my last book anyway. If I keep making high-speed midnight runs to cool out my head, there's no way to avoid a bad crash." Yet "we have a bit of time before that—& as soon as I get settled in my new writing room I'll send a better letter. I'll also send some money—when Silberman sends me some. OK for now—see you in the fall."

What he didn't spell out was that in the past six weeks, since the very end of April, his pregnant wife had been bedridden.[39] Not knowing that she was prone to miscarriages, I didn't take literally the invalid statement or that his lawyer Clancy was nearing a nervous breakdown. Sandy's terrible situation would continue till around August. She would endure a lingering buildup to a miscarriage. Hunter kept the household going. This came to light for me only in 2008, when Rosalie Sorrels mentioned on the phone what a good father he was, citing how in this period he looked after his and Sandy's son, three-year-old Juan. Many letters that immediately follow look quite different in this context.

Visualizing him zooming around hairpin curves (which I did), I worried he might have a fatal slip.

On June 22: "M—Good luck with explaining that call—I was

almost dead toward the end. But when I hung up I felt totally jangled by the sudden return to continuity—like a hermit jerked out of a cave & put back on his job at the mill. What next for the nerves? Madness—what else? . . . That Penguin dedication should read: 'To Margaret Ann Harrell.' Or just 'Margaret,' if you want it that way. Let me know. Ciao H."

But this is a well-kept secret. The dedication never got into the book, dropped out in proofreading or who knows, but it was not intended to be omitted. In fact, this is one of Hunter's many red handwritten letters in this period, on his Owl Farm stationary. He did not keep copies of the nontyped letters, as he did of the typed ones, back in his basement in an archive.

10

Jan Makes Noise, Milton Emerges

Meanwhile, Jean-Marie's first book was reviewed by Pol le Roy, critic and professor at the University of Ghent:

> A tight-lipped and a furious one. A bloke, an adven-
> turer. A rebel and freebooter. In many ways, even in poetry.
> . . . The tone is like the man: rash and without illusions,
> almost churlish and alternately of a striking and not striking
> cynical roughness. . . . It remains an open question how this
> raging vagrant of wanton and healthy moral piracy manages
> to rhyme some pious, oh yes, and semi-sweetish things too.
> Nevertheless, from the harsh settlement with life and death,
> many sober sincerities have already grown into striking
> poems. A name to remember: Jan Mensaert. A resounding
> debut: *Poems from the Pawnshop*. Colibrant." (*De Periskoop*,
> May 1967)

In Morocco he was again in a fertile period. By July 11, 1967, with the second book finished, he combined it with his love of composing:

> Wrote the word FINE just five minutes ago. . . . The
> idea of turning the whole thing into a baroque opera li-
> bretto gave me so many new ideas that I had to do the book
> all over. It's become a real classical opera, that is as far as the
> form in concerned: ouverture, five acts with, each of them,
> so many scenes, ballet, interludio, trionfo, arias, duos, trios

up to a nonetto. Called it "slow night on the meander."
There's no plot. It's all psychological, delivery of an obses-
sion with the help of some thirty characters, St. Michael,
Scheherazade, Cleopatra, Orfeo, Titania, a deus ex machina,
etc. . . . It satisfies me at last. But then I've never worked so
hard on a single thing in my whole life.

He explains how he cuts "Dutch to pieces . . . and invent[s]
new words. . . . Am sure about one thing, there's never been written
anything like this in Dutch, as far as weirdness goes. Not weirdness
through putting funny words together—they are everyday words
though badly maltreated."

It was only after his death, through the wife of his publisher,
Jef De Belder, that I saw Jan's letter requesting that his first book be
dedicated to me, with the words *The Result* (that is, of sitting on the
rocks overlooking the Atlantic as he translated aloud). To have one
book dedicated to you is a great privilege. To have two by different
authors at once, unheard of. To have both lost in the accidents of
time is even more unheard of. What could it mean? What secret
principle that could ensnare both dedications and stash them away
in secret places?

In this tight nexus—which, though disconnected and diverse, was,
in fact, besides my own book and job, the center of my life—Milton
Klonsky was beginning a slow emergence from underground. Looking back at the vivid details now, I feel just as much starry-eyed in a
ballroom. To me, who had not known him in the 1950s or early '60s,
Milton was the same: inspiring, dedicated, a genius, who burned
the midnight oil, then strolled out to bars. These Village locations
he took me to included Casey's Chinese restaurant, to meet perhaps
Terry Southern (coauthor, *Dr. Strangelove or: How I Learned To Stop
Worrying and Love the Bomb*, *The Cincinnati Kid*, *Barbarella*, *Easy
Rider*; novelist: *Candy*, with Mason Hoffenberg, etc.). Or we'd stroll

over to Bradley's, an East Village jazz bar and grill owned by a former bartender from the 55 dive bar. Or the Five Spot (to hear Thelonius Monk), or taxi uptown. Milton loved jazz, including that of former girlfriend Beverly Kenney, a Billie Holiday-esque singer whose voice sounded in his apartment—over expensive wall speakers out of place in the bareness. But a sprawling library filled towering bookcases in which, till pilfered, you could find a hand-inscribed Marianne Moore and so forth, authors he knew.

In this year Milton abridged an 1894 book, musty, archaic, odd: *Light on Dark Corners: A Complete Sexual Science and Guide to Purity, containing advice to maiden, wife and mother, how to love, how to court, how to marry etc.* (Grove Press). He did not bring out his poetry. But not to be left standing on the wayside, neither did he remain in the dark of no publications either. He transmuted those hours when he sat in a chair in his apartment, reading thick books, into a reputation. He began marching out into the daylight of a name as an editor and William Blake scholar, planting this book at the beginning of a trail. However, he did not exactly condone spending the time ("I didn't need the distraction. But I did need the money").

When the evidence began to come in that he, who, he said, "can write poetry as well as anyone alive," was editing instead (not in addition), he somewhat gloomily but with burning, lucid eyes characterized it as "a way of being tired . . . so I'll ride in taxis instead of taking the bus." No, his job and calling as poet were not satisfied that way. Not that it was either/or. It tickled his sense of quaintness to "resurrect the dead." It added joy, irony, spice to see this piece of history, *Light on Dark Corners*, in existence again. I was proud of it too, though I stood with him in the CONVICTION he was GOING TO WRITE GREAT POETRY.

He said, "Our relationship, we've been over enough; we're a well-worn rug. We've paced up and down it, and it's beginning to show bare in spots. . . . I think your main decisions are made not in your head but in some turbulent dark psyche."

11

Hunter in the Woods

By July 13 Hunter was still not out of the woods:

Dear M. A......

It's ten minutes of seven here and I'm getting wiggy. The past two nights have been wailing hell on the typewriter. I'm putting the bomb to all my writing "obligations," including the Rum Diary. Mainly it's an effort to get rid of Meredith, but I think the whole deck will be cleared in the process. I wrote Silberman last night, demanding all my money. But I really don't see much hope for any peaceful dealing with Random House. Personally, I'd like to stay peaceful....but professionally and financially I can't live with a pawnshop operation. And so much for that. . . .

Everything else is depression. I'm canceling magazine assignments, answering old letters and generally trying to get human again. I'm also looking for other sources of income.

Learning of his piddly $200 "share on a sale of 13,000 a/o April 1," he declared: "Needless to say, I've hired a NY lawyer. We are finally into the real, inevitable shit. Ciao H."

I replied that I'd promised a second round of book-tour notes, which I'd never mail "if I stop to make [them] sound good." So here's "an extra-extra rough page" (three single-spaced pages).

To take a few examples of my notes, when a call-in listener compared the Angels to Nazis, "HST agrees every time. . . . Finally HST stops him: 'How many times do I have to agree?' Caller: 'Say it a thousand times.' Visions of the rest of the show taken up with proclamations of 'Down with the Angels,' then equal time for the other side ('Heil, Barger')."

Another caller, "Disturbed," typically disputed the announcer but tonight patiently waited on line to give "a regular toast: To this fine young man . . . polite, eloquent, articulate . . . You know that, don't you?" Meanwhile, "Jay walking with authority to the coffee machine, a look of service on his face not unlike that of the waiters standing with towels on arms at the L. A. hotel; . . . very proprietary about keeping this privilege for himself, though the announcer was allowed to pour [Hunter's] brandy[!]"

On the Lomax show he was booked with cheerleaders and a serious eleven-year-old boy, who, looking very small, sat at the corner of a table. The boy had spent two years writing a book. I wrote: "Lomax peered over and began to prove what a little thing this kid was: 'Who did your typing?'" Was it his sister? No? a girlfriend? ("A Groucho Marx type scene, laughter each time, and Lomax is no Groucho.")

Finally, the child admitted it was his father's secretary. "The audience loved it, and when they'd stopped laughing, time was up, with only a closing second of seriousness about the book—just time enough (in true 'absentee landlord of the spirit' style) to say how much work it needed." I drew an arrow: "stolen quote," referring to Herman Melville.

Reflecting on a *New Republic* review, I stole another Melville quote: "What madness and anguish it is that an author can never— under no conceivable circumstances—be at all frank with his readers." Then I alluded to a funny scene in which Hunter had explained, tongue in cheek, why we'd slipped away, citing as the reason that it was to change his shirt:

Motto: "For reasons that were never made clear . . ." [he'd said].
(A little nervous laugh, and then . . . bleep . . . no more sound.)

Sometime in here I received an undated collect Aspen Western Union telegram: HIPPIES YESTERDAY FILED SUIT. BILL KENNEDY TRIED TO CALL LAST NIGHT AND EXPLAIN AND DISCUSS YOUR NIXON-LASHED FUTURE.* CALL LATE AFTERNOON WOODY CREEK FOR DETAIL. END PRESS.

Presumably, this referred to the lawsuit filed in California's Federal District Court by folk singer Joan Baez and other conscientious objectors against the Vietnam War to recover part of their 1965 and '66 income taxes.

In early August, Hunter came to New York. Sliding in and out, he tried to finalize the Meredith problem—wrestle the negotiations in his favor, hunkered down, invisible, narrowly focused, blasting his way. *I did not even see him.*

Naturally, this rankled. He came all the way and didn't phone!! But things were deadly. Inexpert as he was in handling the negotiations but forceful in expressing what he believed, he made a mad assault on the bulwark.

It was during this trip (or might be)—I'm not sure of the chronology—that out of the blue his wife telephoned. Nothing could have been more unexpected than to hear her voice—friendly (in no way attacking), which stoked the impression (quite false) that an acquaintance had given me that they had an "open marriage." I was amazed to think she suspected he might be with me. She volunteered that she'd had a miscarriage and that afterwards Hunter flew off to points east—his whereabouts unknown. It sounded brutal. But she wasn't condemning. I mostly listened, unwilling to shatter my privacy. Was he in New York?! My adrenalin surged—panic.

Days later, I received a huge mailing tube, with his "orange portrait"—his face on the *Hell's Angels* cover—and another poster. The orange face took a proud place on my wall. Unfortunately, his elaborately enlarged portrait had been sent by R. H. to Woody Creek "so flimsily [wrapped] that only a carrier condor could have got

---

*As previously mentioned, William Kennedy had been managing editor of the *San Juan Star* when Hunter worked in Puerto Rico. He would later win prestigious awards as a novelist.

it here un-bent." Feeling "ugly" about returning it, he gave elabo-
rate instructions: once repaired, it should be mailed in the tube air
express, which "beats hell out of brown wrapping paper." No, make
that COD—$10—mounted on a board.

"I don't feel like explaining my behavior in NY right now; it
would take five pages....so I'll save it for the phone some afternoon.
After I see if it worked. Which should be 10 days or so." He concludes. "In any case, if you could have hung me on your scales that
morning I flipped out for NY, I wouldn't have registered at all. More
later....H."

I worked on *The End of Obscenity: The Trials of Lady Chatterley,
Tropic of Cancer and Fanny Hill* with Charles Rembar, the First
Amendment lawyer who successfully defended these cases. Two years
earlier, after he argued before the U. S. Supreme Court in *Memoirs
v. Massachusetts*, it clarified once and for all the conditions for ban-
ning a book as obscene, in a ruling that despite appealing to "pruri-
ent interest in sex," John Cleland's 1750 *Fanny Hill*, republished by
Putnam's, was not obscene because not "utterly without redeeming
social value." Earlier, he defended the unexpurgated *Lady Chatterley's
Lover* (D. H. Lawrence). His first cousin and tennis partner, Norman
Mailer, supplied *The End of Obscenity* Foreword.

Jim assigned me to Rembar's law offices, where I'd arrive at ten;
his entire day was devoted to editing. We spread stapled chapters
on the roomy conference table and at lunchtime sent out for deli
sandwiches; around 6:30 we popped into a nearby restaurant, each
drinking one Michelob. We'd examine structural intricacies (complex law procedures detailed in multiple places). A lot of work
accrued from the fact he showcased digressions. About ten I'd go
home. Throughout, I marveled as a secretary typed up changes, and
fresh crisp versions appeared.

After publication Rembar wrote in my father's copy that I had a
fine legal mind. This was satisfying in that my father originally hoped

I'd be a lawyer. One day my father asked me to edit his eulogy on the death of his friend Congressman Herbert Bonner, to be read into the congressional record. As he read he wet his thumb, to turn pages. I started to delete repetitions and he stopped me, pointing out, "This is a speech." I never forgot how astute that comment was.

In Rembar's Acknowledgments he cryptically called me "a lass with a delicate ear." He said *you edit by sound.* I moved my finger back and forth (like a pendulum). Hunter had typed whole books by prized authors, to get the rhythm.

The End of Obscenity won the George Polk award in journalism. The faded review I clipped, from the *Washington Star* by Day Thorpe, unhesitatingly branded Rembar's book "a masterpiece." Thorpe declared Rembar "a writer of such self-confidence that he does not force himself always to stick to the point . . . he feels, I imagine, that a book without digressions is like a house without windows, and he is constantly turning aside to focus on ideas and observations that are wise, or provocative, or witty, or hilarious." He tells us that Rembar "assumes that nothing that is of interest to him will not also interest his readers, and he is right. Every really good writer shares the same conviction, perhaps unconsciously."[40]

It was another Silberman classic. After this (and because of it) I found myself with Milton in the loft of Geraldine Page (the actress) and her actor husband, Rip Torn, with Norman Mailer. I mentioned having tried (and failed) to edit his Foreword. Because of the repetition, if you cut it, the text fell apart. He said perhaps he should have been edited; eventually Faulkner was edited. I found Mailer stunningly sensitive. His fluctuating expressions shifted slightly over his face, modified fragilely to suit precisely shifting accents of the conversation. He was unarmored, *really listening.* Milton, surprising me, was jealous.

On "10/11/67," just before tens of thousands of anti-Vietnam War demonstrators protested in Stop the Draft week, including rallying at the Lincoln Monument and marching on the Pentagon, Hunter announced that he'd finally turned in the *Colliers* piece, overdue, very long—"& 3 times as complicated" as they asked for. He wanted me to "send an honest comment or two." After *To Tell the Truth* people wouldn't give him "as flat & frank" feedback: "We should talk about this sometime—it's a long & terrible story. Sort of 'right is might,' etc."

> And speaking of terrible, what the fuck happened to the dedication in the Penguin paperback edition? . . . Anyway—it was supposed to be dedicated to you. I thought you made that change. Did you? If so, let's make the bastards rectify it. What a sloppy bunch of swine they are. Even the hardcover Jacket is a mess. If you told them about that change in the dedication, I'll raise all manner of hell about it. Let me know—& send a general word. Ciao, H

Hunter canceled the *Realist* piece October 22. Refunding the advance, he put the onus in part on Meredith.* He told Krassner he "recently flew to New York with a heavy club, for no other reason than to crash into [Meredith's] office and whip on him." That was an attempt to prevent his "stealing all my funds" as one of those "young, no-leverage writers who've been conned into signing with his agency."[41]

Confidentially, I'd confided that I intended to leave my job—but had set no definite date. He asked why: "[A]ny switch on your part might affect my contract action, which should come to a boil around the first of the year, when I plan to be back in NY for some dealing.

---

*To me, he wrote that articles were sprawling into impossible length—under one hundred pages felt "like a meatless outline." He was used to having assigned topics, such as by McCarey Williams. Also, books yielded no fixed payment. For a few years he was to flounder, speak of a writing block. As a topic, "the Death of the American Dream" lacked focus. As he tried to stabilize it, it reached tentacles into his articles.

Let me know."

With Milton I attended *The Beard*—Michael McClure's incendiary, poetic play about Jean Harlow and Billy the Kid in eternity—directed by Milton's friend Rip Torn. When Harlow takes off her panties, he rips them in half. In Los Angeles fourteen straight nights officers arrested the actors.

In the off-Broadway Evergreen Theater, a light show preceded the performance, echoing the San Francisco Fillmore production; in the lobby were cages of ferrets and doves. According to the *New York Theater Wire*, "The controversy, in which the ACLU defended the play, seemed to pit an artwork about Eros and the divine against a repressive establishment that was bombing fishing villages in Southeast Asia."[42]

Torn won an Obie. But what I remember was the grand crescendo, when after Billy repeatedly buries his head in her thighs, he slides her dress up, "grasps her thighs and presses his face between them, kissing her. Harlow stiffens and arches backward: 'STAR, STAR, STAR, OH MY GOD—! STAR,'" etc. Sitting close to the stage, it looked to me as if—well, you know. That shocked me.

It must have been about this time that Milton and Rip Torn interviewed each other on TV. Rip was Milton, Milton was Rip. They never let the audience in on the secret.

Replying that he didn't know McClure, Hunter enclosed his obituary of Lionel Olay—which he asked me to pass to Krassner: "I completely blew that article for him. I figure this might be something he could use to fill the gap. . . . Your summer sounds like a fine wild blur of strange action. I'm jealous, of course, but what the hell. Send me a copy of the 'big book,' whenever you get one—maybe page proofs."

He now had a *Ramparts* column, to let off steam and pay rent. But the "writing block [was] worse with every new article. That's why I'm giving them up."

Finally, "I'll probably call you one of these days or nights, for general purposes. I'm feeling a little better today, after spending the last of my money. It was a hell of a job to get rid of $7,500 in six weeks, but I managed. So now I'm back to the nub again, and it feels nice and edgy."

He wouldn't hide out the next trip: "That was a bad situation and I'm sure I was right in avoiding you and everything else that might have confused me. That's not an insult. I wasn't in a very pleasant mood, for a lot of good reasons, and my nerves were on the surface."

November 21, to M. A: "Yeah....that salutation used to be a joke. But then a lot of things used to be funny. I thought my freak-out in August or whenever it was—that quick shot to NY—had cleared things up, but apparently it didn't, and things have gone from ugly to rotten since then. Total paralysis on my part—total loss of communication on all fronts, canceling of assignments, refusing to answer phone, etc.....The Fear."

He had sent me "a novel by a neo-friend named Oscar Acosta" (the to-be Dr. Gonzo in *Fear and Loathing in Las Vegas*). Not having read it, he hadn't "the vaguest idea what I've sent you....but if it's any good, for christ's sake don't tell Silberman about it; give it to somebody else. And let me know."

>   The whole [future book contracts] thing
> is so goddamn wretchedly complicated that I've almost
> despaired of coming to grips with it myself. Meredith
> has screwed me on about eight different deals and there's
> apparently nothing I can do about it. It's become so bad
> and dreary that I can no longer bring myself to write letters
> about it.
>
>   I think you're right about needing a total
> break—not just for you, or me, but as a general principle.
> Especially for people who work around books. What a
> nightmare business that is. Even if I wrote a book about
> it, some 10% agent or editor would steal all the money
> and probably prevent publication. I am gearing down for
> another run to NY, I think, but this one won't be discreet.

I figure to get arrested for three or four cases of aggravated assault. When I decide, I'll let you know. The last thing looked good at the time, but since then it's fallen apart.

        Anyway, it's snowing here—six or eight inches so far tonight, and very white and peaceful. It looks like a long winter. Ciao....H

A postcard December 18: "Leaving tomorrow—tell Silberman to prepare his check book—H." Nevertheless, it was just into the New Year when Hunter flew in.

Jim Silberman had invited Hunter to the most expensive restaurant in town, the Four Seasons—along with Bernard Shir-Cliff of Ballantine and Hunter's lawyer. Around Random House, there were trepidacious jokes that in his great unrest Hunter would show up in leather, twirling chains. The myth *perpetuated* by more than one book is that the 1968 meeting (below) occurred in an earlier year!

In his unofficial biography Paul Perry locates it *in the spring of '67*. He says that neither Silberman nor Shir-Cliff "had ever seen Hunter"; they met in Pete's Tavern—"to work out the kinks in [*Hell's Angels*] and think of a sequel." Hunter wore "a waist-length zipper jacket [with] what looked like a lumberjack shirt underneath." In fact, Perry *conflates the '68 trip with the '67 trip*, in which he promoted *Hell's Angels*.

Even so, Hunter and Jim had met earlier. And Jim recalls no meeting *ever* in Pete's Tavern ("It not a place I went to"). Certainly, he says, not one where Hunter drank twenty double Wild Turkeys.

It was winter-'68 (*this* trip) in which the trio brainstormed—Hunter, as Perry indicated, wearing (he wrote his mother) "boots and my shooting jacket."[44]

In the five-hour dinner Wednesday night they bandied around book topics, in particular "the Death of the American Dream," though according to Jim it was not first suggested then. It was the

result of a phone conversation: "You couldn't have had that kind of
conversation in a restaurant, because it had to be developed. Unlikely
[in a restaurant]." I asked, was "the Death of the American Dream"
his suggestion? Jim said no, that looking at the common thread in all
Hunter was writing, "I told him that *is* what you're writing."

High on the probable-projects list was a quick paperback about
the Lyndon Johnson reelection campaign (killed when in a speech
to the nation March 31 President Johnson announced he would
not run) and a hard cover on the Joint Chiefs of Staff, also called a
Prosecutor's Brief on the Death of the American Dream—neither
of which would in fact materialize because his breakthroughs would
come in *Fear and Loathing in Las Vegas: A Savage Journey to the Heart
of the American Dream* and *Fear and Loathing: On the Campaign Trail
'72.*

Many letters in the Gonzo collection attest to Jim Silberman's
lasting friendship, patience, and consulting role. About splurging
at the Four Seasons, he added that they definitely wanted to keep
Hunter: "Absolutely. The book was a success. He was a wonderful
writer. Clearly we wanted to keep him."

I asked, "Did you perceive a problem about money? Did you
perceive a tension?" Jim: "There was always tension when you said
no to Hunter." Jim said Hunter wrote much more about money than
came up in conversation.

Regarding going through other people to get requests passed
to him, Jim added: "There was nothing complicated about it. He
needed the money. Until very late in his career, he managed to spend
more than he took in. . . . He was using Selma that way [to get to
him]. Which she did."

"But it didn't bother you?"

Jim forthrightly: "It was part of my job." As soon as possible,
Hunter secured Lynn Nesbit as his agent.

Quiet-spoken, Harvard-educated, Jim took the whole situation
with a grain of salt. He said, not critically, "If there was a *worst* way
to see something, Hunter saw it. It wasn't the *only* thing he saw. But

he saw it." Hunter was "immensely talented." And their relationship was "great. It sounds insane, but I never found him difficult."

Hunter and Jim's bond would thrive long into the future. And long into the future, in '86, Jim and Selma were to marry; Selma would run Selma Shapiro Public Relations in the tough world of New York, while Jim would go to Simon & Schuster with his own imprint, Summit Books, and be placed by Hunter in the *Fear and Loathing in America* Honor Roll.* Selma was smart, funny, a very effective R. H. vice-president of publicity and public relations, not to mention unofficially Hunter's agent during this crisis. Jim was a wonderful boss—always aware in the background, hands on. He gave me a lot of rope. We had a lot of fun. And I didn't hang myself. With a lot riding on the trip, Hunter arrived in New York.

---

*Wondering how Hunter got to Simon & Schuster—did he just leave with Jim?— I learned the answer in a phone conversation in 2006. It turned out that eventually Jim left R. H., while Hunter remained behind (under contract). But though articles for it already existed, no book with Random House was "lashed together." So the publisher let Hunter go. His agent called Jim. Soon Hunter was with Jim. And the stopped-up faucet for *The Great Shark Hunt* opened. I don't know how many people know this story. So I'm glad it's on the record.

12

Hunter: Snake at R. H.

Hunter's blue Indigo Snake, the subject of many a tall tale, was bludgeoned in his New York City hotel room by a bellhop—according to Paul Perry's biography. But though having interviewed more than one hundred people, in this particular segment Perry fell prey to wild rumor. The good Doctor, as Hunter was later called, liked subjective accounts. Subjectively speaking, the bellhop murder captured the essence with a different plot. Coming in early 1968, this episode hailed from the time when Hunter became a celebrity, walked across that line of *before* and *after*. He intended it to accompany him up from the Florida swamps—via New York—to Woody Creek. However, this was not to happen. Nothing remotely similar to this happened. It involved my not "keeping the lid on."

Bought at a reptile farm in Florida, the blue Indigo escaped before takeoff. But retrieved (by his mother-in-law?), it followed on a later plane. Upon its arrival at La Guardia, the airlines telephoned Random House. R. H. reacted to the strange development by requesting the snake be hand delivered to Hunter. First of all, Hunter was serious about getting it back to Woody Creek. But secondly, this situation was ideal for creating a tight spot.

Transported by a stewardess, the big Everglades snake rejoined its lost owner at Hotel Delmonico, Park Avenue and Fifty-ninth. On the phone Hunter discoursed on the dire complication of his loose Indigo strolling around an electric-socket-filled room. Alarm in his voice, he stopped to point out that the snake was examining those sockets. I spontaneously suggested he settle it in my office. My position was by now enhanced by the title "Assistant Editor," given by Jim; he said the extent of my work would otherwise look strange to such prominent authors as NBC nightly news coanchor Chet Huntley, on whose book I likewise worked heavily. He said I could not sign a letter making those recommendations with the title "copy editor."

A few hours after my conversation with Hunter a large thick blue iridescent Indigo settled in cozily in a cardboard box with holes, very close to the other copy editors and visiting authors. It was a snug fit. The Eastern Indigo is docile, but it is the largest nonvenomous snake in North America!!

Blue Indigo Snake

Closing the lid, Hunter said keep it tight like that. I admit I was glad to have an excuse that he would surely drop by. Word traveled quickly—a conversation piece over coffee breaks, even for Bennett Cert. Hunter told me the next day, Thursday, it had to eat. I should purchase a brown mouse at a pet shop.

I stared down at the five-foot creature consuming the office cubicle. With the horrendous expectation of a slaughter, I realized the depths of my predicament. I was an animal lover. But I took the unsavory step, and with great loathing forced myself to lower the mouse in. Later I would not have been able to, under any circumstance.

But the snake was disinterested. Lazily it kept its distance. With overwhelming relief at not having a massacre, I yanked the mouse out and phoned Hunter, who offered as a reason: the snake was shedding.

Bundling the mouse back to the store, I never considered that the snake feeding was a test—a prank. But it's years later, and I don't know. However, that crisis passed. Another loomed Friday evening.

Down from Random House was the Fred Astaire Park Avenue dance studio. Astaire himself opened his original school on swank Park Avenue in 1947. Since Random House allowed us to work at home—to meet deadlines—or arrive late and leave late, I sometimes slipped away for a two-hour class. At the moment I was practicing to represent our studio—in beginning waltz and mambo—in the cross-country ballroom competition in Miami, Florida. Friday afternoon I headed over. *Did the snake have enough oxygen? Surely not. Suppose it suffocated.* I worriedly loosened the lid.

Hours later I buzzed the night watchman. As I stepped into my office what should I discover but an empty box!

How was I going to explain? Egads. Hunter screamed at the drop of a pin. But never at me. I'd assured him I could protect his wild beast. Could I get it back? Distraught, I alerted the police. I remember the operator said clearly, "Hold for the snake division." In New York City!? Great, I said and waited. When they arrived, a short stocky guy, searching in holes in walls, spotted a hole near the stairs. Flinging his arm out dramatically, he yelled "Stand back" and proceeded toward it. To no avail. Solemn-faced, they gave up. An officer advised me to post signs in the toilets: BEWARE OF SNAKE.

Warn every Random employee! Before sitting down, look closely into the water. It might poke its head out of the toilet bowl while you're seated. Or standing, for that matter. Check your urinal under threat of dire consequences. Thus, things were set to proceed! The building would be in turmoil. It might slither over to the adjacent archdiocese to pay a visit to the archbishop, the cardinals, and bishops, though I do not think it could have gotten all the way over to nearby St. Patrick's Cathedral, making its way through some watery passage.

Things did not get that far.

Quaking in my low-heel pumps, I delayed telling Hunter. Saturday broke ominously. I returned to look for the blue Indigo.

But disaster struck. The janitor had not been informed about the friendly snake on the premises. What suddenly did his eyes behold? An enormous mass of snake!—strolling unthreatened up the winding marble Random House stairs. His face stark white, the janitor mustered courage. With a great feat of fear and loathing, he got a weapon. And lacerated and destroyed the menace.

Any reader can imagine I was leery of carrying Hunter the report about the guillotining. I don't remember exactly his reaction. According to Jim, he was in a "total rage" Monday morning, to find that the snake he had left for the weekend was beaten to death. Look what lay in store for a wild spirit in the Big City, even just attempting safe passage. It felt like a reenactment of the Man with the Slingblade in my woods next door. I remember Hunter saw the moral—instinct, which he trusted; not so, authority. His fortified Rocky Mountain ranch versus Big City institutions.

The slithering beast had been unaggressive, but the perception of it ambling down the stairs would lead to all-out attack.

Hunter afterwards tipped his hat to the event. On a windy, rainy day at Delmonico's he thought of calling room service for "one of those portable brick-dome fireplaces full of oil-soaked sawdust logs that they can roll right into the suite and fire up at the foot of the bed." Enjoy the sounds through the *open* windows, take a hot bath, and bill R. H., who "still owes me a lot of money from that time when the night watchman beat my snake to death on the white marble steps leading up to the main reception desk."[45] Ironically, kept advised of the blue Indigo's activities, the editors—everyone—had rooted for it. So the act of bravery was greatly mourned, stunning those who learned of it, as the loss of the snake was the first and only time such an event of any remote similarity occurred in the building.

On that visit Hunter came to town armed. Paul Perry says it was a .357 Magnum pistol he brought, before the days of tight airport security. A .357 Magnum can penetrate bulletproof vests; is good for self-defense and deer hunting.

Hunter took expert photos of me holding his handgun, which I prized but lost. There we were in his room. I picked up the gun. And he—hairy legs, dimples, and all—grabbed his camera. I rested my back on the bed and reveled in pretending to be a gangster's moll.

Not knowing he was a photographer, I marveled when, marking crop points, he daringly *narrowed one photo to a vertical strip.* I didn't know that in the Air Force he laid out sports pages.

Perry said Hunter was "snake-sitting for a friend."

But I was snake-sitting. Certainly he did not return to the lobby to find it in chaos—his snake "stretched out on the floor and lying on a bedsheet," smashed to death by a bellhop with the tube of a vacuum cleaner.[46]

I ask myself why Hunter is unforgettable. He had a brand, and it was himself. He left that branding on people. In my experience, he seemed to know you or let you know him, not putting on the gloves but also not putting on the blinders. He later remarked to me how significant it was that he had a public personality before he got to explore it on his own.

From the time of the funny young author who wanted his back cover to display a nude photo—of the back side of himself—to the famous Gonzo reporter, the truthseeker, here's a correction for the record: that with the snake as with other things, the underlying truth (here, anyway) was an attempt to get a large many-colored, harmless but forbidding snake out of the Big City to a ranch in western USA. The snake did not make it. The lid was not on tight enough, when its natural drive for freedom and its curiosity found a way to begin roaming. I hadn't believed it could survive with the lid that tight. We guess, on the other hand, that HST, even with the lid off, as it was, did. Yet I get the impression that in a sense it is also now, with so much information coming forth, that the lid is "coming off."

As time passed I've occasionally pondered, thinking of "levels of truth" that Hunter spoke of, just what were the other dimensions to my insisting on taking over control of his wild Florida Everglades snake in NYC. And that I let it be killed before it could retreat safely to Owl Farm in Colorado. I was responsible. I took it in on my initiative. What had been killed? Was there no symbol beneath it? Was it a purely physical act in contrast to all the other events in my life, which, looked at later, had a symbolical level? Not that what dies cannot rise again, of course, from its ashes.*

A review of Hunter's published letters beginning in 1968—the above period—by Andy Markowitz noted: "The *idea* of Hunter S. Thompson has long since overtaken the actual writer—the startlingly original prose stylist and satirist whose dispatches from the dark corners of American culture and politics definitively chronicled 'The Sixties' and their dank hangover." He said the letters illuminate "that Thompson did a couple of lifetimes worth of living before he turned 40." Reading them sent Markowitz frequently back to the writing from that time period in *The Great Shark Hunt*, "to reacquaint myself with that wild, searching voice. 'I don't know about you,' Thompson wrote to Wolfe in 1968, 'but in my own mind I value peaks far more than continuity or sustained effort. . . . [F. Scott] Fitzgerald spoke in terms of 'the high white note,' which explains it pretty well—at least as far as I'm concerned.' For a while, Hunter Thompson sang that note, in a way few contemporary writers can match."[47]

Though I'd secretly confided to Hunter that I might leave Random House, the decision was waiting for a precipitating event, the assassination of Robert F. Kennedy.

Milton said of Norman Mailer: "There are those who write and those who blurt." He designated Mailer a "blurter," like a kid in a classroom who always raises his hand with the answer. Milton took

---

*Hunter's *Gonzo* account of the story would perpetuate the snake's fame, in 1972. I will report that account when we get to it.

things deep inside, or they just went there on their own, resonated, found a safe place, assorted with other high frequencies, turned into wisdom as in a factory—came out ready-made for print, even in speaking, no exception, at least to my hearing. I always thought it might have been my inner voice speaking when he spoke aloud, saying I was "a mole" like him, identifying with me in that, trying to teach me. He had noticed that molelike quality—probably referring to "The Burrow" by Kafka, the symbol, the image of living underground, not letting on what was in there, a very private person, and when speaking remaining private in some way. But in writing? He used his mind, his intellect to a great degree. He pronounced it too interfering, saying that knowing so much was an inhibitor, that one thought like Emily Post, checking to be sure the words had their—*etiquette*, he said—that so much learning was prone to cripple the spontaneous outpouring, which would be stopped at the door. About Emily Dickinson: "Read the ones with the dashes. They're unsocialized."

Who wrote "like the slow motion of a summer's cloud"? he wondered. He couldn't recall. "Perhaps I did."

"No!" he shouted. "I would have said, 'Slow' is too slow; 'motion' is too abstract." (I remember his cadences.)

Back at Random, Cy Rembar's book came out in 1968, along with a memoir by Chet Huntley (NBC news coanchor of *The Huntley-Brinkley Report*), *The Generous Years: Reminiscences of a Frontier Boyhood*, intended to be the first of his autobiographies. Just after Huntley was *Setting Free the Bears*, the debut novel of John Irving.

On my expense account I sometimes treated authors to a victory meal. Chet Huntley, however, invited me to his Italian haunt. *He* paid the tab—the only one who ever did besides actor Peter Bull. At lunch Huntley recounted political stories (cf., about when Hubert Humphrey wanted to go to the Playboy Club; Huntley, who wasn't a member, managed to get them in; Humphrey gathered the bunnies at his table—only to begin campaigning). How uncomplexed, unpretentious, openhearted, the high-profile Huntley was. Being nearsighted, he asked me to check if that woman waving at our table was Lee Radziwill, sister to Jackie Kennedy Onassis.

John Irving had to be coaxed to New York. He suggested to his editor, the wonderful Joe Fox,* that *they* fly me to New Hampshire. After the touch-ups, I invited him to the Italian celebrity restaurant. Who should exit but Huntley?

He walked straight over, and in that anchor voice that each night began his news show with "Hello, David [Brinkley]," boomed out, "Hello, Margaret!" He added, "Listen to her. She knows what she's talking about." I relished the way Irving's face creased in surprise.

---

*This was the Joe Fox, whose name was given to the Tom Hanks character, the bookstore-chain owner, in *You've Got Mail.* Script writer/director Nora Ephron had been a girlfriend of Fox's. Joe was Truman Capote's editor; when Capote went to Kansas for the death-penalty hanging while writing *In Cold Blood,* he was accompanied by Joe.

13

Oscar Acosta

Back in November Hunter had sent me Oscar Acosta's manuscript *My Cart for My Casket*—asking what I thought of it.

The two first met a few months earlier, in The Daisy Duck bar in Aspen in "that high white summer of 1967," as Hunter recounted in "Strange Rumblings in Aztlan." Oscar came over "and started raving about 'ripping the system apart like a pile of cheap hay.'" Hunter put that down to "another one of those fucked-up, guilt-crazed dropout lawyers from San Francisco—some dingbat who ate one too many tacos and decided he was really Emiliano Zapata." Oscar did odd jobs—washing dishes and construction work—then left. When they hooked up again around Christmas 1968, Oscar was with the L. A. public defender's office. As the only Chicano lawyer in the nation, he wrote Hunter, he represented mostly political criminals, guilty or not.

Hunter used "Strange Rumblings in Aztlan" to comment: "*Most* of my friends are into strange things I don't totally understand." Mostly, he let them be. He reflects, "Who am I, after all, to tell some friend he shouldn't change his name to Oliver High, get rid of his family and join a Satanism cult in Seattle? Or to argue with another friend who wants to buy a single-shot Remington Fireball so he can go out and shoot cops from a safe distance?"[48]

It was through Oscar that Hunter wound up covering the murder case of L. A *Times* journalist Ruben Salazar, the news director of the Mexican American station KMEX-TV. (More ahead.) In *Fear and Loathing in Las Vegas* this Chicano activist lawyer—cast as Dr. Gonzo, the three-hundred-pound ulcerous Samoan attorney—would share "infamous" star billing with Raoul Duke.

It took me awhile, but I eventually sent Hunter my critique of *Cart*, to pass the gist to Oscar but not, on any account, to let Oscar "get hold of" the letter itself.

Two hours before leaving for the Denver airport (to fly to New Hampshire to cover the primary), he *forwarded Oscar my letter*(!!). He adjured him not to tell me he had, but to "[compound] the fiction in case you ever talk or write to Margaret."[49]

In New Hampshire, he took that famous ride to the Manchester airport with candidate Nixon, who wanted to talk about pro football. Hunter inattentively let his lit cigarette hover near the fuel tank of Nixon's Learjet.*

Hunter replied to me February 26 that he changed planes in New York en route to New Hampshire "to follow Nixon around." Returned via Boston. No time to phone: "Besides that, I think your earlier letter hit on something that's beginning to bother me; I think I'm losing my talent for establishing human relationships, or even maintaining them. I seem to be sinking into myself; both talking and writing are increasingly difficult."

Compounding the fiction, as requested, Oscar told me that Hunter had *written* "concerning your comments on the mss." Three letters from Oscar followed. The picture that comes through is complex.

He says February 17: "Both you and H. T. accuse me of moralizing. I ain't going to cop out to the Fifth, but you should know, and H. will certainly be reminded of the fact, that I was a Southern Baptist Missionary in the jungles of Panama for two years." Though to me this was flabbergasting, reports confirm it.

Oscar is "familiar with St. Paul's injunction with respect to retaining one's childish notions after one becomes a man, but the fact is I'm still a soft soap." He mentions a routine of running a mile on the

---

Outlaw Journalist, by William McKeen, describes this event vividly: "The Secret Service had not recognized the threat; it was [aide Nick] Ruwe who grabbed the cigarette from Hunter's lips. Hunter tried to reassure him: 'You people are lucky I'm a sane, responsible journalist, otherwise, I might have hurled my flaming Zippo into the fuel tank'" (121).

skid row sidewalks in L. A., and after that, "I sit in the tub and laugh at myself and at all the coming day's clients; I even poke fun [at] the judges and remind myself that the District Attorney is not necessarily evil because he enjoys putting criminals in jail."*

Despite all this, "I sit there and scrub and look at myself in a handmirror and make funny faces** . . . nothing changes: when some poor sap of a hippy, some dumb cluck of a negro, some pathetic Mexican bum, when they get busted and I can't win the case." Though he knows they'll be jailed for some time, "hell I still take it as I always have . . . like an emotional, infantile sort of guy."

On Hunter's advice Oscar had recently cut a novella down to a short story; "then yesterday I got a letter from him where he said I ought to 'quit fucking around with short stories' and write a short novel instead. (Hunter is mad.)"

He brought up the reason for the letter: "Hunter wrote some of the things you said, and read me a couple of lines over the telephone [*Indeed*]: 'He ended the book as he did, I think, not for the sake of the characters, but for the sake of the idea.'" Oscar suspected the observation was true.

He asked me to please read twenty-three pages of "Perla"— including a passage where an old peddler, Huero, disappears after a rumor that he peed in his field: "Hunter said the story was about 'people are doomed monsters.' But, like I said, Hunter is mad, or at least crazy." He thanked me for reading *Cart*: "You are the first person of any consequence that has."

---

*The editor of *Oscar "Zeta" Acosta: The Uncollected Works*, Ilan Stavans, says he was a missionary while in the American military in Panama. In *The Uncollected Works*, Houston, Texas: Arte Publico Press, 1996, 5–7; referenced in "The Religious Affiliation of Oscar 'Zeta' Acosta," http://www.adherents.com/people/pa/ Oscar_Zeta_Acosta.html. Hunter says it was in a Panama leper colony and that Oscar always fell back on preaching. He was, further, "a stalking monument to the notion that a man with a greed for the Truth should expect no mercy and give none" (*Great Shark Hunt*, 504). Oscar later entered folklore with two publications, including *Autobiography of a Brown Buffalo*, 1972.
**Autobiography of a Brown Buffalo* opens with a semi-self-portrait reminiscent of this passage though more gritty.

From Random House I wrote him to *call me Margaret and send it.* I said I could use some California sun.

Oscar's reply March 7 began on a personal note: "Strange how people create images based on crummy movies seen long ago. I had called you 'Miss' not so much because of nonacquaintance, but rather because of some long forgotten second rate movie. You were fortyfive [*sic*], wore glasses and used to teach school; that is, until you decided a more useful life could be found helping young writers." He'd learned the fallacy of this impression, when "some jackass named Gene McGarr comes along and tells me you are young and pretty. Of such ephemera are dreams made of!"

Hunter wanted Oscar to write a nonfiction book, so Oscar was researching the militant Brown Power movement in California. He wondered if I knew that "the Mexican has joined forces with the Black Nationalists, Stokley Carmichael, et. al very recently [I didn't]." Despite having marched in a Vietnam peace rally with Hunter's friend Lee Beery, I had nil interest in politics in general then (though I do now). My eyes rounded like saucers at what came next.

Awaiting trial, he said, the two biggest Brown Power heroes—Reies Tijerina (New Mexico) and César Chávez (Delano, California)— were debating "whether or not to make the racist scene with violence an ideology."*

Oscar was "attempting to talk them into selective assassinations, rather than indiscriminate rioting; and that as a tactic rather than part of the philosophy."

Saturday he would interview Chávez, who was sixteen days into a fast "(so far)," and he hoped his own "uptight anxiety" would go

---

*This comment is hard to figure. The charismatic Chavez supported picket lines and nonviolent boycotts. He founded the United Farm Workers union. At the time of the letter he was in a twenty-five-day fast supported by Robert Kennedy and others. Reies Tijerina fought for restoration of property to heirs whose land grants had been confiscated by the United States in the Mexican American War. In March 1968 he was probably in prison. Later that year he led the Chicano contingent to a Washington DC march organized by Dr. Martin Luther King Jr., who was assassinated before the march.

unnoticed, though he was "trying not to pay too much attention to poets and presidents nowadays, listening more and more to myself the older I get."

Logging in at over a million Mexicans, East L. A. had the largest concentration of them in the world outside Mexico City. Poorly represented, the Mexican had it even worse than the blacks, he went on. After laying out statistics, he hopelessly alluded to "El Gabacho (White man)['s] . . . 'instinctive aggressiveness' . . . he cannot give the means to a minority if he believes that in the long run he'll be, or his society as he knows it, will be wiped out. It is what Lorenz spoke of in On Aggression, perhaps the most important book I've read in my life."

He closed: "[Y]esterday I swam in the ocean under hot suns and white foam, in Venice West. Thanks [in advance] for reading Perla. The sun is on its way."

Meanwhile, I'd won the cross-country championship—in beginning waltz and mambo—in the Fred Astaire competition in Miami. For a theater arts contest, I was rehearsing a spectacular ballet bolero with lifts, in white tights and a Grecian tunic. I luxuriated in being raised onto the shoulder of my teacher—from which I'd dive down in a flip, once cracking a rib. I liked falling. It felt like mini-skydiving. So I regularly walked the few blocks from R. H., on Madison Avenue, to Park.

Ballet Bolero

In this period I received a priceless post card from Milton from Greece. On one side was Ulysses tied to the bottom of a ram.

After the Trojan War, Ulysses sailed home to wife Penelope and son Telemachus. But diverted by winds to the island of the Cyclopes, he and twelve men were penned in a cave by the one-eyed giant Polyphemus, who began to eat Ulysses' men. With quick-wittedness, they stabbed the giant in his eye with a hot spear. Tied beneath Polyphemus's sheep, they fled the blinded Cyclops. Milton wrote:

Dear Penelope, *This is one way out but how do you escape the Inner Eye?* Have been caged by a bird on Myconos; now in Rhodes. Goodbye to Istanbul! Soon to work with director Ted Kotcheff on—yes!—Madame Solario! We are all twitched by invisible strings. And you? Will land in N. Y. C. sometime in June, I guess, and then . . . Ulysses.

P.S. The world is square if you live on the edge.

— 14 —

The End of R. H.

The year 1968 thundered through with two assassinations—of Dr.
Martin Luther King Jr. and Senator Robert F. Kennedy. June 4, Kennedy was at the Ambassador Hotel in L.A., celebrating having won
the California presidential primary. He was a close second for the
Democratic nomination. However, suddenly, in the kitchen, greet-
ing busboys and waiters after his speech, he met the unthinkable:
Sirhan Sirhan shot him at point-blank range. Twenty-six hours later
he was dead: killed in his prime like his brother JFK.

Triggered by RFK's death, I felt sharply, intensely: *I could die
abruptly, at any moment.* I had to turn in my resignation; I *had to
leave* to finish my book!

I was seized by the intent to finish my book, begun in Paris,
which from the moment I met Milton had him as the star—alongside the totally fantasy protagonists Anny and Joseph, who in a counterpoint role illustrated my love of the physical, which I poured into
these imaginary figures, thinking, however, that they were not like
me at all. The real me was the writer, who at this moment loved her
job but it too was consuming. How long could I keep burrowing
myself in my apartment on weekends, which were the only time I
had to write, and yet I also needed downtime? During the week we
often had overtime.

And I knew full well that the unconscious, which gives us wonderful passages for the printed page, is demanding. My unconscious
practically memorized the manuscripts I worked on; it charted about
every sentence where a writer used a significant word *and reused it.*

I had grown sure that this compulsiveness to do right by the manuscripts I edited was confiscating my unconscious.

But how would Jim take it?

I held the decision all night, and I think it was the very next day, before my resolve weakened, that I went rather fearfully upstairs into his large office, where he sat familiarly behind a big old-style office desk with leather top over wood. I didn't want to let him down. Not to mention my parents. Turned out he was already prepared.

Recently he refreshed my memory. I asked him now, forty years later, if he was caught off guard. He paused a long time. Then he mentioned Arthur Murray. I said, "Fred Astaire, yes." Well, he'd made the connection when I started spending a lot of time there that I was about to leave Random House.

"I thought that you were getting ready to move on to what would be the next part of your life."

He said, that day, that I had mastered the "quintessence of copy editing." The head copy editor, it turned out, was not at all pleased. Instead of treating me with kid gloves, she was businesslike, insisting I stay on for two months, which was reasonable, and that all manuscripts be wrapped up and everything out of my desk on the dot of the deadline. That shouldn't have been an issue, but it turned out to be.

Meanwhile, a letter zipped in from Hunter—oblivious to what had transpired.

Two days after Robert F. Kennedy's death, Hunter wrote me, enclosing fan mail from Carol Hoffman.[50] Also his unmailed second reply to her, which said he owned a silver mine in Mexico and had gone there—so not to send money. Hoffman had written him as "one of the nineteen million bored-to-tears housewives in this nation!" To offset tedium, she'd enrolled in a fiction-writing course and wanted pointers from him. She speculated that respectable townspeople would be so shocked if the Angels passed through: "they would die instant deaths!!!!" *Hell's Angels* played to her overwrought imagination. She pictured time with them as a blast every day.

In reply he told her he "broke a lot of goddamn faces." And that presently two Angels were cruising the country, perhaps near her. Also, he'd just punched a stewardess and put an interfering person's eye out and needed a legal-defense donation. He said, "Yeah, nothin but crabs between me and whatever I want to hurt."

Dear M. A......

Somehow the initials seem appropriate, considering this wild heap of garbage I'm sending....867757463544 pO58¢$***$@.....or which I was in the process of sending 3 ½ hours ago when I heard a car in the driveway (at 2:30) and now they just left..."they" being a guy I barely knew last summer and a girl and a carload of hashish from California—and who showed up here foaming desperate because he'd just heard that the sheriff and federal narco people were waiting for him at his apt. Two hours of wild speculation hiding cars (2) and a little brown suitcase worth as much as I could make with a best-selling novel. Speed freaks are hard on the nerves—jabbering about heat on the (Sunset) Strip, borrowing shovels to bury the evidence along with $12,000 in small bills. Jesus—summer is coming on again; I can feel the mad vibrations.

Anyway, I want you to mail these two letters for me—from New York—but I thought you'd like to see the background on my letter to Mrs. Hoffman. Notice the dates on her letters; they came like hailstones, one a day, ruining my breakfast. Each one worse than the last, a raving nightmare. I left my final note to her un-sealed, so you can see the end of the saga. At least I hope it's the end....and that's why it's crucial that you mail this from NY. I can't allow this woman to find out where I am. So please mail my "off-to-Mexico" note after reading it. The xerox copies are a souvenir for you; they are a stark and terrible example of that secret madness I was talking about in the book. I was talking sort of abstractly when I wrote that stuff, projecting in the sense that I was using a novelist's license for journalism.....but jesus, it's true. They're out there, and they're real....and they're tracking me down. You can't imagine the wild shit that gets forwarded to me via RH. The other letter came in the same mail with one of the Hoffman poems. Show it to Jim, along with my reply suggesting that he contact him (Silberman). This may be the Great White Southern Dope Novel.

Don't get these things mixed up. All I want you to mail are the two (entirely separate) replies that are already in envelopes. I only left them open so you could read them before mailing. Hang onto the xerox copies and the original Stanford letter. We'll all be involved in a terrible lawsuit if you mail xerox copies of that woman's correspondence back to her. But it struck me as right and necessary that you should see this awful evidence of that syndrome I was talking about. This is really the nut of the whole H. A. book....jesus, when I read this woman's first letter I thought "No! goddamnit, I can't humor these freaks any longer...." So I wrote what I considered a cruel and final letter. I figured the worst thing I could lay on her was the prospect of a visit by Terry and Tiny, plus a demand for $500.

....and you see her reaction. The "rising tide" is worse than I knew*; the iceberg is about to flip over and dump all these freaks out of hiding. That stinking arab in Los Angeles; the losers are coming out of their passive cramp, five years from now Sonny Barger will run for president as a moderate. The "new Barger."

Hell's Angels spoke of "weird flotsam on the rising tide, Giant Boppers, Wild Ones, Motorcycle Outlaws" (120).

Another terrible prospect is that Carol
and Shirley will mail me some money and set me up for
a mail-fraud bust. She sounds serious about it, and if any
money arrives I'll send it to you immediately so you can
return it to her with a very rude, severe and wholly imper-
sonal letter....saying perhaps that I've been put away somewhere, for my own good, and that any further letters from
her will result in the whole file being sent to her husband.

But maybe she'd like that. Her husband
must be worse than she is. Where do these people come
from? How can they stay alive? Thank god for the American
Dream; if it weren't for that I might think these freaks are
real. (I have at least fifty letters like her first one; they keep
coming, day after day, now that we're into the paperback
audience.)

Christ, it's nearly 7:00 & I have to get
to bed. Unless I get arrested before noon, I face about six
hours of brutal bike-climbing in a few hours. Forcing a motorcycle [a dirt bike] uphill over logs and snow and rockpiles
up to 14,000 feet. For no reason or profit. No sense at all.

Oh yeah....Oscar Acosta called yester-
day; he asked about you. He's the lawyer for that Brown Be-
ret case in LA. [Senator Eugene] McCarthy gave him $8000
to defray legal costs. And Lee Berry is writing some very
good pieces from Paris for the Albany Times-Union. Bill
Kennedy sold his novel to Dial* and I just finished building
a beautiful log fence in Woody Creek. That's the news
for now.

---

*Bill Kennedy emails, "In 1968 I sold my first novel, *The Ink Truck*, to the Dial
Press, and it was published in 1969. Hunter never read it, or at least he said he
didn't, and wouldn't. This I took as his response to my negative critique of *The
Rum Diary* in its old version. I told him he shouldn't publish it, and he didn't, in
that form. He cut it substantially before it saw daylight. It had its moments, but I
thought it was still a mess."

I told Hunter I had resigned, and his reaction was doubtless by phone. No letter to me mentions it. I explained the decision in terms of starting a "second life." But letters from him pick up again only in August. And my memory, unfortunately, is no help here. So we have a little hiatus.

In August, Oscar wrote again, complete with fantastic logo:

He reveled in being enthusiastically, passionately appreciative. I was "a fantastically excellent reader"; he was "most grateful. I've not ever had anyone go over my stuff like that before." Agreeing the end of his story might be a "cop out," he questioned Huero's "refusal (Job/like) to curse God." But "That's the way the fucker is. It's only in sex and race that he seems to get churned up . . . Huero having neither, . . . he never swats at the nats [*sic*] that gnaw at his eye. I guess I'm caught up in that Pauline thing of victory in death (Oh grave where is thy sting!), which is something that I don't intellectually believe in, but I guess in many ways I am." Unfortunately, he added, his subject was always himself—therefore required introspection, which he hated.

He was immersed in the Southwest Mexican American movement, so revisions would have to wait. As to disinterest in his Brown Power book idea, he compared his movement to "the Blacks"—saying the two had different approaches to the same thing: "we're all lovers and poets, and still the Big Inkwell In The Sky won't write about us [Mexican Americans] or publish what we write about ourselves." He'd told Hunter he would have the Prime Minister of the Brown Berets motivate the *NY Times* editor with a threatening letter. But Hunter remained silent.

He closed with a lovely account of having tried "to send you the sun last March." In various stores he searched "for a pin of the sunburst. The face with the rays around it." When he eventually located a department store that carried it, they had to put in an order. A month later he was notified it was there, went in one week later, and it was accidentally sold.

Then the most gloriously appreciative flowery ending: "Were it possible I'd send you the whole ball of fire. It's devastatingly hot out here. Smog burns eyes red and grey is the universal color. Dulls the minds of an already dead people. Which is to say that I dislike L. A. down from the pit. A sullen gloominess, a dullness, unhipsville, boors and bores all of them. But it's where my action is for the moment. . . . Like right now I have to prepare for a press conference. Margaret, thank you for reading Perla."

I would stay on at Random House, wrapping up, till August 31. Now we have reached the beginning of this book, with me backed up against the deadline to be out of my office. My procrastination or extracarefulness meant I had my desk to clean out, because I spent the earlier part of the day still tidying up manuscripts. Dusk fell. I stayed late. I thought I might literally be there the next morning when everyone came to work.

And then with a fresh breeze at my back and the stars twinkling overhead, I made my way out of the office, not shutting the door one last time because there was none—in a jumble of feelings, happy, sad, and carrying in my belongings Hunter's letters.

I was back where I began three years earlier, just returned from Paris, where I went to start my book and did, sitting in seats sat in by Hemingway and others (Baudelaire, ...). What next?

15

After Random House

The Democratic political convention in 1968 was no less violent than the rest of the year. In the volatile atmosphere of nationwide anti-Vietnam War demonstrations, Mayor Richard Daley issued a shoot-to-kill order in April.

Because President Johnson had decided not to run for a second term and Bobby Kennedy was dead, there was not yet a presumptive candidate for president at the Convention held in Chicago, August 26–29. Hunter attended, naturally, with R. H. press credentials.

Time magazine reported, in "Daley City Under Siege," that to secure the Convention, the nearly 12,000-man Chicago police force "was ordered onto twelve-hour shifts; 5,650 Illinois National Guardsmen were called up for possible reinforcement, and 5,000 more Guardsmen have been put on alert; 7,000 Army troops were preparing to move in."[51]

Daley was prepared, *Time* said, "for full-scale insurrection." Vowing that no one would take over his streets, he had cops on every corner and inside every block downtown in the Loop. At the Convention headquarters, the Conrad Hilton Hotel, "federal agents were assigned to the roof, main corridors, kitchen and service areas." Vice President Humphrey, Eugene McCarthy, and Georgia's Lester Maddox were staying there—along with three of the delegations. "Other agents were on round-the-clock duty outside the candidates' suites, checking passengers debarking from elevators." Across the street Hunter and McGovern's hotel, the Sheraton–Blackstone, was likewise protected: "Press photographers were warned not to shoot pictures through open windows lest they be mistaken for snipers."

To no avail in preventing violence. Using tear gas, barbed wire, and clubs, riot police manned checkpoints. To make matters worse, 75% of the cab drivers and many electricians at Illinois Bell were on strike. In a Party rift, Vice President Hubert Humphrey became nominee over antiwar senator Eugene McCarthy.

For Hunter the ensuing savagery and mayhem that shocked the country was a crystallizing moment.

In writing me from Woody Creek September 20, he mentioned that (as a high school senior) he'd been involved in an incident that prevented his graduation and redirected him into the Air Force. I'd read it involved theft.

"I checked out your rumor (about me) & my informants tell me I was locked up for that, once...cigarette stickups in the park, except the record calls it 'attempted rape.' Damn weird in retrospect." He suggested that "you embellish the tale as best you can, and pass it along. Selah."*

He cited the riots in the Windy City as the opening salvo in his new focus:

> Shortly after I talked to you I went
> to Chicago for the Convention and my head began spin-
> ning a million miles an hour—on the American Dream
> book, which I'd nearly abandoned when I talked to you.
> Silberman arranged for my press tickets, hotel room, etc.
> . . . jesus, what a horrible scene; the Fourth Reich out in the
> open for the first time.
>   Speaking of things I owe—I'm enclos-
> ing a birthday present of sorts, as a down-payment on some

---

*In the Cherokee Park stickup Hunter, in fact, was in a car with two friends when, to bum a cigarette, one got out. But that guy robbed a guy, stealing his wallet. Whether he then told them when he returned is unknown. The victim reported the plate number. The influential parents of the other two sprung them. In view of Hunter's minor police record, the judge ordered either jail or military enlistment. Hunter chose the Air Force, where he became a sports reporter (Neville Blakemore and Porter Bibb in *Gonzo*, 18–19).

money I recall oweing you (e? Owing? No, that can't be
right.) . . .

As for [*The Rum Diary*], it's still in
limbo. Nobody's ever read it for un-biased pros and
cons—neither Silberman, who says I should rewrite it, nor
Shir-Cliff, who wanted (a year ago) to publish it as is. I've
given it some thought in the past few weeks, and I've about
decided that it would be dishonest to re-write the book
in any serious way; it seems like it would be the same as
giving it to a ghost-writer—an older and balder HST. So
I'm thinking very seriously of doing a surface, mechanical
re-write job, mainly cutting and clarifying, rather than re-
thinking. Which brings me to the...ah...point: which is how
much loose time you have on your hands these days? How
would you like to read the Rum Diary and tell me what
obvious faults you feel should be dealt with? I could send
you one of your xerox copies. Let me know.

He was "writing bags of pages every day on Chicago"—for a
book tentatively titled *Eight Years on the Road to Chicago; Notes on
the Death of the American Dream—or, once again, Which Side Are
You On?*

"How—to change the subject—is your second life shaping up?
I'm curious; the whole idea fascinates me. I'm also curious about
the book you've been writing. Send word—and Happy Birthday.
Love, H."

In Chicago he felt he'd witnessed the end of the 1960s:
"[R]ammed in the stomach with a riot club in Grant Park for
showing a cop [his] press badge," he admitted that "what caused me
to tremble when I finally sat down behind the locked & chained
door of my hotel room . . . was not a fear of being beaten or jailed,
but the slow-rising shock of suddenly understanding that it was no
longer a matter of Explaining my Position." Those in charge were
not "actually listening." Though not a demonstrator, he was in shock
that there seemed now no use in protest or engaged argument; the

new power was "born deaf and stupid."[52]

To Jim Silberman: "Chicago was the reality I've been theorizing about for too long."[53]

Describing the convention, he brought in his alter ego Raoul Duke, who told him, "You're a traitor to your class . . . sneaking in here to drink with the over-thirty generation." Hunter's answer: "'I'm thirty,' I said, 'This is my time, my perfect moment'"[54]—slipping in a hint of the lyrics of "And I Like It."*

Incidentally, my father was a delegate. He found it so rattling that it was the one time in his life he had a drink *after* a meal, rooming with his friend Senator Sam Ervin, not arrested and hit in the belly but nevertheless disconcerted.

In leaving Random House, I began teaching ballroom at the Park Avenue Fred Astaire. Thinking it would allow time to write in the mornings (at last), I reported to work about 1:00 p.m. But got home about 10:00, so I was no better off on the writing front. Further, I didn't enjoy asking students to purchase expensive class packages.

Dribbling in were letters from "the Belgian poet," now faring miserably. With two books published, he'd resigned the teaching contract in Larache. Alas. Unable to write in Belgium, he was a salesman for a French aperitif. Not comprehending his relationship to alcohol, his uncle secured the job as first step up a corporate ladder.

In diametrical contrast with the Moroccan bliss, Jean-Marie wrote: "Am listening to La Traviata for the 437th time. Don't know what it is: precocious senility, I guess. But I like the stuff. Makes me cry romantic tears. Never knew I was a romantic. I am. Found out lately. I finally accepted that Dubonnet job, you know, and what with the hardships of business life and the likes I somehow feel I need an antidote. That's why you can find me walking on the Tirlemont [his home town] moors on moonless nights if you take the trouble to come over and look for me."

He finished: "So here I am, working, I mean the real thing, the

---

*From Duke will come Uncle Duke in Gary Trudeau's *Doonesbury* comic strip.

one God had it about when expelling Adam from the gardens of Eden. Thought I knew what he meant when I was at my dear Colegio Moulay Mohamed ben Abdellah [in Larache], but I realize now that was still very close to the gates of paradise. Oh and ah! how I despise myself for having fallen so low."

Gone was the happy-go-lucky artist. In its place, Malcolm Lowry. But the letters continued his practice of saying the most traumatic things in the most untraumatized way. While his storytelling was delightful, it was perplexing the way he distanced himself from the actual physical experience while being fully the center of it, to reexperience it transformed into art. In my conversations I referred to him as "the Belgian poet."

I had fled Morocco—fearing the ramifications of being sucked into that environment, where the will appeared to be turned Off; the tap of vegetating, On. Still, I confided anything I felt like. After all, he set the bar of no-holds-off-limits, no-confession-too-outrageous-to-be-permitted. I tried to make myself sound interesting. But I made no attempt to keep up, as how could I?

The writer disappeared into oblivion but not without a few struggling gasps, he was "becoming quite a case. . . . studying the ceiling, my feet and the tortoise in the garden for the last hour and still don't know what to write about. Am having a bloody Mary to stimulate my alcoholic muse. And indeed, wings start fluttering around mine ears. I'm sad as usual, plucking my lute to the moon on the pinnacle of the highest tower, but this time at least I know why. Had a tooth extracted and felt exactly like I felt on my last birthday: diminished and older."

He desperately missed "the boiling crater of Art in my breast," the "God of the pure Joy, I have named Apollo." Perhaps, when heading a tour through Morocco in July, he would stay. Meanwhile came the blow-by-blow account below, which created a jumble of emotions:

> Had another drink, which emptied my bottle of vodka (ave censor, communistus non sum) and diminished my

typing abilities, it seems. Don't feel high, though. Was desperate last week. . . . Well, to go on, I ran out of hashish and was wondering what to do next to pass my time away with when I remembered I had a small box of kif hanging around somewhere. Made hashish myself . . . A grain of the stuff and I pass the gate of Allah's paradise, romping in blooming meadows, playing the flute and pursuiting [*sic*] frisky goats. Enough to last until the 1ˢᵗ of July.

Am feeling high now. Can see you walking in Larache [Morocco]. Me and the breeze. Wow! That's poetry. The roses in my garden and the bumble-bee in my head. I'd better stop.

I'd ask you to answer immediately if I didn't know that was the surest way to make you put off. Remember you always would start walking slowly when you had to catch a bus or had to be somewhere at a certain time. . . . My tooth starts hurting with all the ice in my drinks. How's your novel? You're so silent about it. Want to know. Wish I had you around to give me ideas for writing one myself. Felt in Larache I would have been able to write something absolutely great with your help. Love, JM.

I was sent *The Rum Diary* on the old typewriter pages, in manuscript. One of the first to ever read it!! I thought it needed work. But the handwritten revisions, I *really liked*. The online biography "The Great Thompson Hunt—Roads—The Life of Gonzo" records: "1968—HST attempts to publish *The Rum Diary*, his Puerto Rican novel. It keeps bouncing and eventually he gives up after having a Random House secretary steal it back." However, yours truly was never a Random House secretary. No, it was not factually like that.

It was a time of several forks in my life. Attempting the impossible, I applied to the oldest artist colony in the country. Founded in

1907, MacDowell Colony in Peterborough, New Hampshire, was overlooked by Mt. Monadnock, a favorite of Thoreau, Emerson, and Mark Twain, not to mention Colony alumni such as Thornton Wilder.

Most of my authors recommended me. I asked Hunter—in one of few surviving copies of a letter from me to him, October 23. I began: it was "dues day, and I'm soliciting paragraphs":

> My second life has taken a strange, unforeseen turn right off at the start. I'm using all my wits to get myself into MacDowell Colony. Supposedly you have to be "established," but with enough good words dropped by the right people, I think I can get around that.
>
> So when you are looking into your past some evening in the very near future (like tomorrow), do you think you could possibly come up with just a few words about an uneditorial approach to editing; they're interested in originality—I mean, a mind that turns itself to fiction—rather than in criticalness, although both together would be okay.
>
> Surprise—I'm sure you didn't expect this. And I didn't either. But really, I'm not asking for much. On the other hand, if you're all tied up, don't feel obligated.
>
> Also, if you want something to go on, read the next page (which is only one style I fall into; when the characters change, without my intending it, the style changes too—though not obtrusively [next page no longer attached]).
>
> There are a lot of themes, but I guess the main one is having a rapport with one's life (as you said, "This is my life, I'm . . ."). There should be a question mark after that. Also some certification to "my."
>
> In different ways each character relates to this, but particularly Patsy [Paula], who begins, really, as pre-herself; or a me that has inside it a still-born "I." Getting the "I" out is quite a problem.
>
> There's a lot more, but when I start going into this, I feel

like you about the Chicago book; I have to write mailbags.
How is that coming, by the way? And what did you decide
about the <u>Rum Diary</u>? Maybe you're waiting for that letter I
said would be coming in a few days, which I still haven't written, because this isn't it.

More clues: the contents are—
- Vulnerability Established
- Lilies Festering (from Shakespeare); ⎰ <u>both refer to</u>
- In Some Like Chamber (from Yeats)* ⎱ <u>the whole poem</u>
- Brown Spots Hatched
- A few themes: dishonesty can be a way of being honest
- As if never happened-ness
- Coming to things with the clairvoyance of an old man's
  reasons before an old man's time
- The chemistry of explosive opposites
- Unlived lines (i.e., in our bodies—dying without living
  them)

Hunter asked for more details "since my luck in recommending
people, things, or ideas to unknown parties has been 1000% bad."
He wanted to know: "What happens in the 'Colony'? . . . should I
mention a specific work in progress (of yours) that I'm particularly
happy about? Which one? Or should I just say Miss Harrell's novel,
one of the most interesting pieces of prose I've ever laid eyes on...' Or
what? I'll say anything you want, and if you send me a draft I'll retype
it, sign it, and send it along."

"In any case," he added, "I'd feel better about the whole thing if
I knew what they wanted to hear. I think I understand what you're
after, with the notion of 'unlived lines' but I don't see any sense trying to explain that to something called the MacDowell Admissions

---

*The reference to "In Some Like Chamber" is from "Meditations in Time of Civil
War." "Lilies that fester" comes from "Sonnet 94."

Committee."

Finally: "let me know what you need and I'll do it. If you're in a
hurry, send a suggested draft to me at the Continental Hotel (yeah)
on Sunset Blvd (8401 Sunset Bl. Hollywood 69) where I'll be from
Nov 3 to Nov 10." Ah, yes, the hotel where we'd rendezvous'd. So
he was there, surrounded by and referring to many memories just
between the two of us that popped into my head. Very important to
me was that after reading that miniscule sample, he took the whole
thing seriously; he didn't throw my pages against the wall or rip them
apart. Had they passed muster? He ended: "I expect to be back here
after that...working on a weird and maybe unworkable book that I
can't explain. OK for now. H."

Nightly news anchor Chet Huntley generously provided an
"enthusiastic recommendation" for "the editor" of his book: "Her
approach to editing, her feel for language, and an incomparable ear
are altogether amazing. In short, I would consider it a personal favor
if you can accommodate Miss Harrell in any way."

Likewise, Charles Rembar: "The combination of qualities
she possesses is rare—a remarkable sense of structure and balance
along with unusual creative imagination. Her feeling for language is
extraordinary. . . . Her leaving Random House means that a number
of writers will publish books less good than they might have been.
But this loss will be far more than balanced by the writing she herself
will produce."

The die was cast. I was in a Three Coins in a Fountain moment,
from my point of view in hindsight. What would the verdict be?

November 17 (from Hunter), in a letter addressed to the Arlington
Hotel, West Twenty-fifth Street:

          OK....I'm on <u>your</u> side. What the hell
are you doing in the Arlington Hotel? And what happened
about that fellowship (or grant, or prize) that you asked me

to recommend you for? I'm ready with the recommendation—all I need is the words, or at least a rough draft.

    I just got back from L. A. where I spent
a good bit of time with Oscar (Acosta—the Mexican law-
yer/writer of yore). If you're really serious about a Second
Life you should go out there and become the Executive
Secretary of the Brown Power movement. Oscar has become
its legal voice, strategy-haggler and publicity-seeker. . . . You
should immerse yourself, as it were, in the Chicano commu-
nity and become a sort of latter day La Passionara.

    In any case I'll be in NY sometime in
early December and I'll try to locate you through RH.
Meanwhile, don't get arrested.....H

Oddly, Hunter's letters have become the way to chronicle-ize
these years.

    "I'll try to locate you through RH" makes me rapturously recall
a Saturday when—in the dance studio teacher's room—the wall
phone rang. It was Hunter. Likely, this trip to New York took place
December 6–8. ("And maybe Dec 5 & 9, too."[55]) Would I come
immediately to One Fifth Avenue (then a hotel) just off Washington
Square Park?

    Absolutely. "But I'm in a dance marathon till 11:00 p.m.!"

    "A *marathon!*" Hunter answered. I could feel the wheels of his
brain bemused. *"Come afterwards!"*

    I arrived. He was alone, but the next day friends flocked to watch
the NFL on TV and drink beer. It was a completely magic interlude,
including the fact that he waited for me till after eleven. With more
than a twinge, I watched him leave.

    The events below are so tightly packed, in truth, many directions
were there at once, as when a congestion shatters a single direction.

A very dramatic letter slid in, like a baseball player putting his
foot onto the plate. It was from Jean-Marie. It fulfilled his role of

inevitably, touchingly—with the right balance of art and reality—
providing something so extreme it sounded like fiction:

> 27 December, 1968
> [Strangely, this is the day of
> Jean-Marie's death, the suicide
> that worked, twenty-two years later.]

My best wishes for a merry Christmas, a happy New
Year with plenty of American astronauts on the moon and
food in Biafra and a meeting between the two of us . . .
I've actually started thinking of those Spanish dances [he'd
promised to write] . . . I am thinking so well that I've got six
of them all clear in my mind and a little more confusedly
in my fingers. The left hand is pretty rough. But it's hell to
write them down. I've started with the simplest one and my
eyes are dazzling with little black spots and bars and keys
and stars of inspiration. I'm afraid it will go with my olé-olé
music the way it went with [letters, etc.] . . . It may sound
like something made by an Eskimo on a six month's night
after reading the *Alhambra Tales* . . .

And now for the wild story of my last adventure . . .
when I took the train to Athens the intention wasn't to pray
on the moonlit Acropolis but to get to Santorini and have
a very good time—lived with six Swiss air hostesses whom
I happened to get acquainted with and which were spending their holiday there in a wonderful house built with so
many terraces on the caldeira—and then, when money and
air-hostesses were about to be going, committed suicide, or
at least tried very hard to. It was very well planned; drank
a gallon and a pint of ouzo, hid with a couple of spiders in
a dark corner and cut a couple of veins and nerves of my
upper arm. Blood came spouting and I felt very happy. And
then something happened which I still can't explain. I wasn't
suffering, I wasn't afraid of dying—that's what the ouzo was

for—I was lying there and felt very comfortable and satisfied with the things being, went on drinking and singing
and thinking of Thailand and Morocco and Margaret of
the good olden days which would never return and then
suddenly I got up and ran for the nearest-by place. Not for
help. I realize now that I was only looking for human com-
panionship, that I didn't want to die with only spiders for
company. Got to a café—this thrilling story takes place in a
spooky little hamlet high up on the warm and misty cliffs of
an exploded volcano, where Hephaistos dwells and Orpheus
sings his songs of woe—and was a sensation. I enjoyed it.
The owner ran for the Swiss girls and they came and hugged
me and kissed me and spilt their sweet tears on my face and
took off their stockings to bind off my arm and never suc-
ceeded, while all around me people were quarreling about
what had and hadn't to be done. I forget what happened
next. Didn't faint, it was the effect of the ouzo. When I
sobered up. I was lying on an improvised operation table
and still bleeding. I confess it most humbly, I panicked.
Inwardly, that is. I was sure now I was going to die and the
sensation isn't an agreeable one when one (hm!) isn't drunk.
The blood kept spouting and filling the back of my trousers
and everybody was trying to stop it and touched the cut
nerves and it was like having your 32 teeth extracted at the
same time while my heart was hurting like hell. Then finally
when I was hearing the angels singing and the bells toll-
ing and a Swiss girl asking for a glass of brandy something
very much like a doctor came and said abracadabra while
burning herbs unknown to me and stopped the bleeding.
It was morning by then and I was to be flown to Athens
but somehow nobody knew where the helicopter who was
to do the job was. So I was carried down the 600 and so
many steps to the port, was put on a ship where everybody
thought they were bringing a corpse. Because of the sun
they had completely covered me with a blanket. In the

Piraeus hospital nobody seemed to know narcotics had been
invented some years ago and so, while they were sewing
up my nerves, I swore I would never try to commit suicide
again and die as an antique dealer. Stayed in the hospital for
about a week and then decided to go to Prague . . .

Had a rotten Christmas, though a white one. Slept.
True to my oath I've become an antique dealer. . . . Never
met so much vanity in my life . . . The shop has been open
for not even four weeks and I've sold for 3.000 dollars
worth, representing 2.000 dollars benefit. I would never
have expected it . . .

Going on with my life story and resuming it, flew
from Athens to Prague and got there one day before the
Russians did, fell in love with the Czechs, an admirable lot,
came back to Belgium, after having been thrown out by
the Russians, and am busy having my arm reeducated. This
seems to be a failure, it's lamer than it ever was. Even my
fingers, of which I still had control one month ago, are giving it up. Yesterday I've tried to record your Spanish dances
in a simplified version. It was laughable. Am smoking tar-
filled cigarettes now hoping for a lung cancer which, I am
told, is the less painful species of cancer being . . .

Burned my last novel, which may have been good,
my last poems, which were excellent, I know, would
burn my paintings but they weren't worth the trouble. A
Gotterdammerung mood.* It's rotten to have an artist's sen-
sibility and desires and ups and downs and not to be one.

To me this letter was a little treasure: How could the experience that should have accented pain accent humor; that should have
accented transformation instead accent close observation?

I saw this lifestyle inside "the artistic personality"—though I was
huddled down, secretive, throwing my black coat over my manuscript

*From Wagner's opera *Twilight of the Gods (Die Götterdämmerung)*

pages on the floor if Milton came to the door unexpectedly. No one could even see the sheets of paper.

At Columbia University I had loved a passage in Henry James's *The Ambassadors*—in my paraphrase: *"Live, live, live, it's a mistake not to!"* More recently Milton had mentioned—in joking warning—"the lineaments of unlived lines."*

In my book I played up his self-portrait as a "teabag steeped in life" (or that he had a "face like a creekbed"). I named the character Robert—not for (but in that way *like*) Robert Penn Warren, who one day walked past my office, his craggy wrinkles in full display.

Alternately, I very much *thrived—and still do*—on ideas. Milton noted the "metaphysics of your structure."

Loosely based on myself, Patsy (later Paula) was cerebral. The imaginary Anny, for all her conformity, was close to her sensuality. She pondered bolting from her marriage.

I briefly recounted the incident of the young Patsy, stalked at sixteen (as I'd been) by the Black Knight, who cornering her in the school hallway among the lockers several days in a row squeezed her breasts outward to the public to create a "spectacle for the masses." The mystery concluded upon, that my unconscious enigmatically flipped to the surface, was this: "Such a memory is a Lazarus / to which one's own self can be a Christ."

Still without recognizing that these characters might connect intricately in me, I found their juxtaposition interesting.

But could I trust my unconscious, which I was following in art? Could I trust my *instincts*? Was I—in my unconscious—"good"? Looking down from the *dizzying heights through the screenless* windows of my Columbia University dorm, I'd been astonished at the thought that just to "let go" might mean falling out(!)

New Year's Day, Milton took me to the opening of his friend Rip Torn's now cult shocker *Coming Apart*. In it, psychoanalyst Joe Glazer

---

*Perhaps from Rilke: "That which finds no expression in his steps and limited swing of his arms comes in exhaustion from his lips, or else he has to scratch the un-lived lines of his body into the walls with his wounded fingers ['In Regard to Art']."

(Torn), in a rented apartment, covertly films his mental breakdown: through a mirror the hidden camera captures his sexual encounters with unsuspecting women as he disintegrates into a reflection.

When I asked Milton what people would think about my applying to MacDowell, he said no one would be surprised, "Everybody knows. It's written all over you. You have an ink-stained soul." He said that sight unseen, they'd know I had talent. Why? "There must be some recompense for the kinks in your psyche."

About us: "I only break away from things slowly, like when you're a kid and have a bandage on your knee. You have to remove it slowly," he said.

"I have to go through these endings slowly because I don't like to be separated from my illusions. I don't like to think I could have been that wrong."

I was still sometimes seeing and always being dazzled by Milton, whom I had, as he put it, "corrugated into this frozen kaleidoscope."

16

HST: The Outer Banks,
Jean-Claude Killy

I am being extradetailed here during this countdown to a major event. Since the dance marathon, when I'd stayed at Hunter's Fifth Avenue hotel, I'd begun dating an Italian ballroom instructor, a lanky, sophisticated Gambino. It never occurred to me to think of the Mafia. He was undereducated with a burning desire for philosophy. During breaks he'd pull out Martin Heidegger and we'd fall into discussion.

Unexpectedly, Hunter phoned again into the dance studio—this time from his hotel room in DC. I heard opera in the background. I asked did he like opera? (Yes.)

The hectic pace in DC was "getting to" him. ("Life runs mean & fast in [Washington]," he would soon write. As in "an armed camp," it required "a condition of constant fear."[56])

Now he made the most sweeping suggestion ever put to me—to meet him immediately at Cape Hatteras, that unspoiled Outer Banks sandbar off the North Carolina coast. I drew in my breath—another "high white note." California all over again.

I felt there was something game changing about it—definite. Not that the game could really change, but important.

From hindsight, it took some effort to reconstruct that he had been at the Nixon Inaugural ceremonies. Hunter's grand nemesis, his whipping board—recipient of his most colorful power outages—had "no inner convictions," said Hunter (of Nixon), a condition he genially equated with no soul. But for more reasons than that, the 1968 Inaugural was unpalatable. In "Memoirs of a Wretched Weekend in Washington," he spelled it out.

The "weekend was a king-hell bummer in almost every way." Minus any shred of peaceful protest, antiwar demonstrators threw rocks, firecrackers, and garbage.

In savage infighting, peaceful demonstrators were offset by shouts of "Two-Four-Six-Eight. Organize to Smash the State." Some wanted to defile the flag. In a preview of his suicide note thirty-six years and one month later he jotted, "No more singing, no more speeches, farewell to all that."

His reason for attending was "mainly to be sure it wasn't a TV trick. . . . impossible that it could actually happen: President Nixon."[57]

However, I digress. He wanted to slip off to the dangerous "Graveyard of the Atlantic"—with me. Be intimately stranded on a sandbar.

The sign to say *yes* glimmered. The salty air I loved smelled of lung-opening freedom. A reminder of waterskiing on the Pamlico. No boardwalks or bustling nightlife. A history of sunken ships, wild horses. Blackbeard the pirate. The black-and-white-striped tallest lighthouse in the US, "The Big Barber Pole."

Stormy seclusion. Fiery sunsets from a private deck—hand in hand on a beach . . . a starry night. He cut through every inhibition in a sheer, stark invitation from this master of romance and, at the moment, genuinely agonized man. Head-spinning visions of sand in the toes, dolphins, sperm whales. But most of all, the raw, bare fact that we were there. However, . . . there was Dominic Gambino. Yes, but what about my heart? Dare my heart say *no*?

When going out romantically I was monogamous, for as long as my feelings lasted or felt hope. (This included Hunter, though I'd never told him. Why would I? It would be silly.) So it had been a big decision to start dating Dominic. I felt the jolt of electricity—I felt its *life-changing crescendo*, the high-splashing waves. He was listening, ready to warp fly to the rendezvous. But I never went.

Refusing him for the first time, my heart down at my heels, I said I could not get away.

Now, with the 20/20 vision of years and years, I imagine that two planes of reality, as it were, were in play, two sets of truths. What synchronicities would the one have unfolded?

In a Letter to Herr Editor, *Aspen Times,* dated the seventeenth, Hunter, back in Woody Creek, wrote that he'd been "called to Washington, yes. . . . For an event of massive importance, a Medical First. . . . Heil! The first chief executive to grow from a dropped pile." He continued: "and finally the Big Day, which I attempted to witness, but was driven off the parade route by a hail of garbage. Those *schwein* will pay, and pay dearly. We have ways."[58] This letter also bemoans the "soldout valley."

Another way he put it: "I went to Washington for his Inauguration, hoping for a terrible shitrain that would pound the White House to splinters. But it didn't happen; no shitrain, no justice . . . and Nixon was finally in charge."[59]

If one tries to untangle the sequence, that period after leaving Random House was truly congested—the space-time cramped, different directions congregated toward different sequels. However, this call was a benchmark.

Dominic was soon gone. He looked like a model, with slinky Italian smoothness. But he took me inside the smoothness. He too leveled with me, as I demanded in a relationship. He lived with another girlfriend but said I was his soulful companion; he would drop her if I would commit, which I wouldn't. So he was often not there. When he stayed over and the cockroaches fell from the Arlington Hotel or Shelton Towers ceiling, wherever I lived when this happened, instead of freaking out, embarrassing me, he took it in stride—showed me how to deal with it. I sometimes bought us Dom Perignon champagne for the room. When I couldn't sleep, instead of saying it bothered him, he stayed awake too; we'd watch a late night movie, he said; turned the TV on. *Sayonara.*

By incredible coup, I was admitted into writers' heaven, MacDowell Colony beginning in March. Each Colony fellow was assigned a cabin (nestled in 450 acres of New Hampshire woods). With a basket deposited on our porch at lunchtime, we spent the day undisturbed, in isolation, if we wished.

I became friends with translator Willard R. Trask, winner of the National Book Award, who appeared fifty-fivish but—unbelievably —was nearly seventy. I was impressed by his translation into English of oral poetry (by African pygmies, etc.) and his best-selling classic Giacomo Casanova's *History of My Life.**

Sky high, I wrote J. B. Rhine. Offhand (not feeling it bold), I alluded to the correspondence between Shelley and Keats. I had no cares, a totally supportive background, bird songs, forests, icicles on the window as I looked up from penning what felt like a perfect page.

I also became friends with a greatly admired author, Tillie Olsen. Recommending the *Diaries of Franz Kafka* to me in particular, she left them outside my door. One night we were walking in the woods together, just the two of us, and saw a spectacular display of the Northern Lights. I remember how her intense spirit threw her to the ground at the sight. For my surprise going-away party she read from *To Tell a Riddle*, with burning eyes that looked up from the pages of "I Stand Here Ironing." Willard read his poem "The Day You Shall Be Dead." As if I already knew *that* moment. Clearly the heaviest of hammer blows.

Parallel-ly in April, unknown to me, Hunter was in New Hampshire to research "The Temptations of Jean-Claude Killy"— about a twenty-six-year-old retired world skiing champion newly turned celebrity endorser. The piece would be published March '70

---

*Willard's classics include Amazon.com best sellers even today, such as *Joan of Arc: In Her Own Words*, based on letters, trial records, and eyewitness accounts. Willard listened to birds, searched for rare orchids, and thought I was a "true writer," which was encouraging. I still wore little heels and took care how I looked at the Colony dinner table, and I never forgot how he appreciated that, telling me that "few people try to beautify the world."

in *Scanlan's Monthly.* In the same magazine his Kentucky Derby piece would appear in June. I don't know in what mile radius this New Hampshire energy field was, but it had us both in it.

In the red hot stimulation of MacDowell, the golden glow when the mind races and ideas fall through the air to land just right, I considered my first book almost finished—the goal inches away. You could stand on top of it. It came together.

I later saw Anny as an archetype, the shadow of Mary, the imaginary *human* side of the Virgin, not the least in that I innocently named her husband Joseph. My Milton character Robert had elegant scenes with Patsy (later Paula). In what appeared to be their last evening together he complained: "You can't turn on and off like that"; she "thought he was Apollo . . . treated him like Humpty Dumpty . . . '*When I kissed you tonight I felt a passion in you, and it astonished me.*'"That scene continues:

> He had to tug to get every word out.
>
> "Tug." Yes. If she was talking about anything important, it was so— He stopped for a word, as if grasping for everything yearned for—"glazed."
>
> The poet in him, the little boy, his wistfulness and refusal to be defeated, broke through every barrier of her resistance. "But not *so* glazed," she said.
>
> "No. We're—what's that word?—*Aesopian.* We pick up hints quickly."

When she announced she might stop seeing him:

> "For the last time, now maybe you can understand this. I'm an ironist. You've never played with me. I want to play with you, on the highest level.
>
> "And one thing more: there's a touch of melodrama in this. And we should avoid those Third Acts. I thought you

didn't like them. There are all those raven people. And I'm
not one of them."

The book virtually finished—I thought—was there anyone I wanted
to see again? anything I *had* to do before I died? Well, I told myself,
make a list and start. I would not like *never* to meet Jean-Marie again.
There are people who intrigue you whom it doesn't feel important to
see again. And others, the contrary. Though I had no logical reason
or even romantic reason, I *had* to see him again—it just felt important. Everything mysterious about him made him perfect for my next
character: so cloaked, so irredeemably self-destructive—yet daring,
creative, brim full of *aliveness,* spontaneous, hidden. Beneath everything, I just couldn't figure out how the obviously rational part of him
justified his irrational, dangerous behavior; I was always interested in
psychology, and I didn't see what made him tick—deep beneath the
surface. But I didn't think of him romantically at this point; he was
that oddity that no one could box in: "the Belgian poet."

He'd been in the far background, a tiny speck. In writing him,
my most insecure self got a chance to wield the pen, download,
dump, test stories—and insecurities. But he began to draw into the
foreground when Dominic became unpredictable and Hunter (out
of reach in any case) was silent.

The restless, jump-in-a-plane, impulsive side of myself handed
me an ultimatum.

This very fidgety side of me—who didn't like to wait around for
Dominic to appear or my next step to materialize—took a stand, put
her foot down, invited herself to Belgium.

At least, that's one way of presenting it. For my young inept alter
ego, he was almost a Life or Daredevil mentor. But to be kept in mind
is that the part of me dazzled by these stories was below the surface in
my awareness, in the way that Jean-Marie was distant in geography.
Was this her view of what SHE might look like if given my strength
behind her choices—allowed her own "lived lines"? It wasn't, to be

clear, the content of the stories that dazzled me—some of which I rather dismissed—but the sheer fact that he allowed himself so much freedom to *be*—*be anything: a decision between himself and himself.* On the one hand, to fly to Belgium was just a spontaneous, merry, carefree impulse but one I could justify as a return to the continent where I had begun the book; only, this time I wouldn't start by sitting in Paris in a café; I would have zeroed in, in Belgium, on my next interesting character for a novel.

From MacDowell, I wrote to ask if Jean-Marie would welcome a visit. A letter confirmed he would. But now his state was even more alarming. I was about to fly into the mouth of "the Big Bad Wolf."

Why did I not call this next letter revolting and be done with it? But that was it: he was exotic, like Tahiti to Gauguin. I couldn't have imagined liking such a man in person as he described himself below. But the fact that he could describe himself, be that objective about it, added an extra level to it all. Who was the observer? In any case, the trip was all set, and I used selective memory in re-creating him, accenting what I wanted to from such epistles, attributing the rest to an overfertile imagination. He had to be exaggerating. Else, how could he be so different from the man I remembered? I was tuning in not to the man who did these silly things but to someone else, larger—I'd say the soul—who invented him to begin with, having all these levels, including the writer who wrote it all down. He began by describing a cocktail party in a garage:

> Very sophisticated thing and I played my lines beautifully, at least at the beginning. I don't know if you've ever heard me play sophisticated lines; I'm really great at it, distant, detached, condescending with mysterious half-smiles, mentioning my meeting with Queen Sirkit with just enough of a whisper in my voice to make people believe we must at least have had a secret affair, breaking off the story of my expedition down the Me Nam, at exactly the right place so nobody guesses it never took place in its entireness,

and everybody being convinced it's only my natural mod-
esty keeps me from giving them the more dangerous details.
Plus an occasional C flat sonata by Paganini which has such
a unique pizzicato in its larghetto or a quotation in Sanskrit
which sets people gasping with admiration. This was at
the beginning. After my fourth glass of Scotch I suddenly
realised [name omitted] was extraordinarily good-looking.
I forget if you've met her; she's the kind of girl who can
look like one of Cinderella's sisters with a hangover and a
skin-disease in the morning and like a Botticelli Madonna
at night. Well, she was looking very much like a Madonna
last night. So I asked her to show me her apartment, which
is on the roof, and made love to her, which was quite difficult because of the kind of dress she was wearing. By that
time all my sophistication had gone and I was boiling over
with medieval romanticism. When we got back downstairs
[her husband] was nasty but very discreetly so because of all
the high-priced future customers carousing all around. So
I helped myself to some more whiskies to help me hold my
temper but the effect was not the one expected.

He argued with the husband, it seems, and woke up in his parents' car: "The end was classical, the vomiting included. In fact, I'm
becoming quite an alcoholic. . . . And that brings me back to another
night. . . . You were skeptical already about my brain concussion and
some other items. Well, take it or leave it, as you like. Anyway, here
goes a true story." He then described being in a Brussels bar and
getting caught by accident in the tail end of someone else's fight: "It
took the doctors only ten minutes to come but the [Brussels bar]
looked as if a whole household had been slaughtered. Six stitches to
stop the bleeding. . . . Another night, coming from Brussels with the
last train and being pretty loaded, I fell asleep and didn't awake until
35 kilometers past Tirlemont. Having no money for a taxi and still
not very conscious of realities, I decided to walk the distance."

He described a perfect start:

a cold, windy, snowy Wuthering Heights sort of night, a
deserted and pitchy road, fairies and goblins dancing on
the rooftop of old farms and sirens singing in the faraway
woods. Then, after an hour or so, I started sobering up and
the sweet voices in the woods grew silent, and the elves and
fairies started throwing snowballs at me and I began to feel
cooler and cooler and more miserable every minute, and
then suddenly I knew all the things Napoleon must have
been through in Russia and I felt a very brotherly sympathy
for the chap. It took me five hours to get home.

For money to return to Morocco and buy a café, he was trying
to sell a "genuine 14th century statue, over two and a half feet high
and in white Gobertange stone. . . . If I had been in Morocco in May
I would have had you stay with me and we'd both have written a
masterpiece and have become immensely rich and famous."

He invited me to his parents' new house in Tirlemont instead:
"quite old and quite big with priest-holes and staircases behind secret
panels and ghosts and spiders. . . . you must come."

The letter gave a blow-by-blow account of what I called his
"Tirlemont syndrome." I was well aware that he was slight of build—
skinny really. Not the brawling type. His anecdotes added pinches of
lack of reality—which I did not take literally, though I did not think
he was lying. It was some kind of surrealist panorama, a theatre of
the absurd, or complexity that put freedom above all else, without
fear—really contradictions everywhere. I guess I didn't understand
how if I resonated with him so greatly on some things, I was completely and irrevocably out of resonance with him on others. So what
was I missing? He was, as said, the main character for my next novel.
So, part of me thought.

Having written him that I now had definite travel plans to France,
I received in mid-April at MacDowell a very enthusiastic enticement:

Slide: Jan's Room, Tirlemont (Tienen)

"I will be in Belgium in May and I pray the Gods, the sun and moon and St Christopher to send you to Belgium. I'm surprised you didn't realize that's what your Northern Lights meant: go to Belgium, go! . . . Wire me the time of your arrival, and I will forget about the letter you promised me and which you seem to have such difficulties with. See you soon.

"P.S. Why should you bite?"

I returned to Greenville, North Carolina, to find a letter from Hunter that was hilarious and bittersweet. He'd had no thought of visiting me in New Hampshire but, as my letters in March '69 pelted his house, had to go there on assignment! I suppose and quite rightly he bore in mind that our relationship not in any way infringe on or damage the rest of his life. Even had it been platonic, which it wasn't, it had dangerous elements.

Hunter broke silence April 27: "Dear Wiggy....All your rude and accurate comments on my general behavior patterns and other senseless movements have been logged, pondered, and thoroughly culled for self-improvement hints." (I don't remember what I'd said.) "Perhaps you wonder why I haven't sent a reply to anything recent.... well, I'll tell you":

By some incredible coincidence I found myself assigned by Playboy to fly in and out of New Hampshire for a ski story [on Jean-Claude Killy]....and more or less the day after I ordered my plane ticket, your first letter arrived with the Peterborough N. H. postmark. Then another, and another, all in the space of five or six days. The result, of course, was that Sandy [his wife] began climbing the walls—refusing to believe that there was ab-solutely no connection between these two New Hampshire phenomenons. Incredible treachery of fate; I was damned for a sneaky rotter, without ever leaving the house or even thinking about anything weird or elliptical. Consequently, I flew into NH and out again like some kind of per diem

FBI agent, spending most of three days in an airplane seat or at least in airports. Feeling guilty for being alive, guilty no matter what I did—doomed to a life of guiltless guilt.... chalked off for a philandering masher while sitting alone on airport bar stools or wandering around that awful ski scene with a drink in my hand and my head screaming "Help— get me out of this horror."

Anyway, I barely recall it. Although now I have to write an article of some 3500 pages on the subject—Jean-Claude Killy [and his sales endorsements]—if only to get the $400 guarantee, in lieu of $2000 for a happy, acceptable, Playboy-style article. It was due Friday the 25th....and now, on Sunday the 27th at 4:57 a.m., I haven't even started. I have a lot of notes and tapes, but nothing on paper. Which means, of course, that I have to quit this rambling outburst and write at least enough to get the $400 guarantee. How is your own madness coming? Your notes indicate a creeping disintegration of mind and personality, a life given over to strange herbs and drugs [wrong]....unholy visions and sporadic hysteria. I can't tell if you're writing a book or dashing off notes on last year's windblown leaves, tossing them off like notes in old wine bottles. Well, fuck it....I'm too drunk and incoherent to write this or anything else. Drunks and junkies are asleep all over the house, and Oscar Acosta arrives tomorrow. I <u>must</u> get this goddamn Playboy thing done. So........ I trust you'll put the enclosed souvenir to good use or maybe skip it across the nearest river like a fine flat rock. Meanwhile, why don't you write me some sort of straight/fact-fat thing and say what kind of action you're into. Jesus....I'll write something else when I get level again.

Ciao....

Hunter

This was a little hard to reconcile with the fact that I still wrongly believed in his and Sandy's open marriage.*

I call the letter bittersweet. But I wasn't callous. I didn't know the facts. Had I known, I would probably still have compartmentalized the two relationships. But I would have known a little more the sensibilities.

In answer I told Hunter I would be using a Shelton Towers, NYC address only till June 1. But not why. I'd returned to New York once again as a ballroom teacher. On May 21 came a confirming telegram from Leuven, Belgium: "WIRE TIME OF ARRIVAL MEET YOU IN LUXEMBOURG BET ILL RECOGNIZE YOU JEAN MARIE." Hunter meanwhile answered on May 19, with an envelope stamped the twenty-first:

> Letters are all I seem to be able to write these days, and I seem to be losing my grip even in that area. The Killy thing was a bomb from the start, a stupid, wasteful thing to work on—very much a Playboy project: fat expenses, degrading research, and rumors of fat payment totally canceled by the necessity to write acceptable bullshit* [Hunter's footnote: *still unfinished on the desk—<u>my</u> desk]. It was Playboy, you'll recall, who rejected the first chapter of the H. A. book when it came to them in the form of an article—along with parts of other chapters.

He went on: "What's happening with your book? And with you after June 1st? I am ready for general street-warfare by Sept. 1st. And I guess it's about time; we may as well get down to it. OK—send a line when you sense movement."

---

*In a recent interview in *Gonzo*, Sandy (now Sondi Wright) acknowledged she'd been unaware of Hunter's relationships; learning of one, she thought he broke it off: "I really, really couldn't have handled the truth. I could not have handled Hunter going out with all the Jerome cocktail waitresses and everybody else. . . . I would have cracked up. I almost cracked up when I found out about the one" (98). But from her other comments the one she is referring to appears to be a quite different relationship than mine, years ahead.

Handwritten on the back: "It's 6AM." He was "Drunk and ill-tempered—looking forward to an appearance later today at a Creative Writing class at the local college—life has become a weird joke—the other day I got a check for $16,000—which I spent for a pasture. Angst is cheap these days."

The "pasture" was Owl Farm, purchased at long last—$10,000 down—with his royalty check and "fine haggling." With the local real estate market spiraling upward, he bought it for $77,000 but valued it at $100,000. Owning it brought peace of mind that his home wouldn't be sold under his eyes. He also bought stock, religiously avoiding AT&T. Ten miles from Aspen, the pastoral Owl Farm included a ranch-style log cabin with basement that stored his archives, a smaller house, and soaring view—plenty of room for his peacocks and Dobermans. It was his "land-fort," or "fortified compound."[59]

The Killy piece, canned by *Playboy*, was embraced by *Scanlan's Monthly*, cofounded in 1969 by Warren Hinckle III, executive editor of *Ramparts*.* This would be in its first issue. (The magazine reached a 150,000 circulation but lasted only nine months.) On June 1, which it was too late to explain now, I was off to Belgium.

In "The Temptations of Jean-Claude Killy," Hunter recalled his most vivid memory of the experience. It was not of Killy. Around midnight, in a bistro at a New Hampshire ski resort, he suddenly heard the drummer/lead singer begin to sing the brand-new Creedence Clearwater Revival hit "Proud Mary" ("Rolling on a River"): "He was getting right into it, and somewhere around the third chorus I recognized the weird smile of a man who had found his own rhythm, that rumored echo of a high white sound that most men never hear. I sat there in the dark smoke of that place and watched him climb . . .

---

*On assignment with *Playboy*, Hunter followed Killy around during his endorsements—for a grand total of one hundred ten pages.

But Hunter discovered that if he wrote honestly, it would offend *Playboy* advertisers and potential advertisers. After commissioning the article, *Playboy*, courting Chevrolet ads, turned it down; in a two-to-one vote, the article's editor "deplored" it (*Gonzo Letters* 2: 195).

far up on some private mountain to that point where you look in the mirror and see a bright bold streaker, blowing all the fuses and eating them like popcorn on the way up."[61]

With limited space, *Scanlan's* deleted the last ten pages. But Hunter fought back: The omission left him, he said, "with a bloody axe in my hand and no apparent reason for the heinous crime." He shrank the end to two and a half pages, including this paragraph. At the same time to Jim Silberman, as a reason for the delay in turning in his next book, he cited a love of writing enduring work, that is, in stone.[62]

17

The Tirlemont Syndrome

I boarded the plane almost as a lark, anxious with the status quo, fidgety, needing movement. Switching to action mode and intuition, I wanted to find my next character. Who else but "the Belgian poet"?

Little did I know what waited ahead.

Donned in trench coat, managing to look both aristocratic and whimsical, Jean-Marie met me at the Luxembourg airport. I'd flown on a low-cost Loftleioir standee system—seated at the last minute. The plane refueled in Reykjavik, Iceland. Instead of relishing the anticipation, he had beforehand staged an unsuccessful "Belgian suicide" with pills and was still in a weakened condition. For the first time I looked into the eyes of someone close to suicide—a tragic creature whose "flaw" was his drive toward art, I thought. This made him appear quite different from the magical invulnerable creature who controlled his world in Morocco. He was, in my eyes, taking long strides toward becoming "real," showing who he was under the fantasies he'd strewn about, the typically "normal" levels hidden somewhere underneath if there at all.

I later thought that around Jean-Marie I was as if hypnotized. In those few times when he removed his tinted glasses, I noted that his gray eyes had white geometric designs. I could not see other viewpoints. His became intensely the only one. My heart did flips. Gone was my intention to study a character.

We boarded the train ticketless. When caught by the conductor, Jean-Marie elatedly slipped through his grasp with a show of artificially broken English. Promptly he led me into his eighteenth-century house in Tirlemont (located in Flemish Brabant, and the name of the town in Flemish is Tienen). Though the family was not rich, their home had incredibly high ceilings, chandeliers, antiques everywhere—Louis Quinze, Beidemeir. "A lute has burst," I jotted. "It burst inside me."

In the short, low oak bed with head and foot panels in which I slept, Goethe had slept, he said, while visiting the local inn. World celebrities including Mozart had in fact bedded down in that inn—which is today a town archive/museum where Jean-Marie himself would have a retrospective one day.

I was struck by a depth not apparent in Morocco. Gone was the happy-go-lucky indomitable spirit, replaced by someone who could be grim-faced, unreadably, moodily silent, deeply introverted.

Slide: In His Biedemeier Chair

In his antique shop for a tête-a-tête with me—when nicely settled in, the mood just right, his eyes sparkling—he asked abruptly,
"Did you ever have a wild love?"

He confided that when he fell, he was "Crazy in Love"—almost
as if it were a brand. He said stop him now. He was writing *The Aziza
Story* about a tragic great love of his now dead.

To get him out of the slump, I encouraged him to apply to teach
French in Algeria. A job was open. He got it.

Though he was too much a "doomed" poet at that time for much
progress on the romantic front, I returned to New York forever
changed. I decided to find work in Algeria myself. Wanting Chet
Huntley's view, I went to his broadcasting booth in Rockefeller Center but arrived minutes before airtime for *The Huntley-Brinkley Report*. With a broad smile, Huntley waved me in amazingly, heard me
out, and said that if asked, "I would recommend you for a job at any
US embassy in the world." Then the buzzer sounded to go on the air.

No longer the least bit interested in Dominic, I quit the Fred
Astaire Studio definitively and—unemployed—sublet for free Milton's apartment while he went to MacDowell Colony.

Accordingly, in July I received one of Milton's rare, treasured letters: "I see you with your cryptic beauty and your redheaded talent
like two heavy suitcases, one in either hand, running down an end-
less underground corridor at Grand Central Universal Sempiternal
to catch a train going God knows where. You'll always be just in
time, I guess." In contrast, Nina had written him, describing me as
"'subdued and self-possessed as Midwestern girls must have been a
generation ago'—which should give you a chuckle." He'd been writing "Poems, thank the Lord."

He would return in August, and I intended to be gracious. But
he threw a wrench into my plans by walking in unannounced in July!
My hair was in rollers.

We got off on the wrong shoe, but remaining in his living room
temporarily, I wrote: "I looked at his face as he slept, having to stay

over two nights—nowhere to stay—after he returned. His lips were poked out, big, like a bratty child; even then I was thinking how in sleep . . . stealing upon a person in sleep . . . one usually steals upon his virtues." I found a new lodging, returned to pick up my suitcase, and told him this relationship made me feel like Sisyphus. He paused and grouped his words into perfection: "If you must think of yourself as the Sisyphus stone, the only way I can possibly get rid of you is to pulverize you and let the wind blow you away." I walked out elated because of the way he crafted the words. No better pleased with him, though. The very contrary. I decided he was "ugly" and "bad."

I moved back to North Carolina, with "Robert" still packed in a book.

"Even now," he had said, "you could change it all with a word."

Laboriously looking for a focus, Hunter was working into his next manuscript. By July 27, '69 he wrote a letter to R. H. to be forwarded, as I'd moved around—from my Greenwich Village apartment to Arlington Hotel to MacDowell to Shelton Towers Hotel, to West Fourth Street (Milton's) to Greenville, my fate being decided. What would the future hold?

Dear Alabaster Editor (Copy, etc.)
attn: M. A. Harrell, nee Random House

    ....what the fuck are the "horse lati-
tudes"? I've heard the phrase for years and never known
where they were. And what the hell do you know
about them?
    ....anyway, I think I may have just
rooted up a job for you. Silberman seems to agree
with my notion that you should do the gut-work on
my new bomb—which he calls the Death of the American Dream, and which I call Silberman's lame idea for a
Thompson book.

....either way, I'm stuck with it. And I recently wrote Jim to say that I had so little faith in the basic idea that I felt the need of a copy editor who wouldn't need three months or so to see me clear....for good or ill. I foresee enough extra problems, without having to cope with the shock reservoirs of such as Barbara Wilson. I'm sure she's an excellent person & I like her well enough, but the idea of her coming to grips with this freaking monster of a book I have on my hands here is more than I need to cope with at this time. Anyway, J. S. seems to agree that I need the heavy assistance of somebody who's already been over the first hurdles, and his last letter (7/7) says: "I agree with you that it would be terrific if (Margaret) could work with you on the AMERICAN DREAM and as soon as she actually gets to NY, I will talk with her about it...."

....so why don't you give him a ring? I am sitting here on about 400 pages that may or may not be fused into book-structure by the time this gets to you. I have plenty of copy; my only problem is lashing it into a book.

Sounds easy, eh? Well....I guess I hope so, but I'm not optimistic. Talk to Jim and get a true sounding, then send a line—straight and wholly professional, reflecting the final truth that in the end we are all salesmen.... and also candidates for survival. Ciao, H

18

Hunter's "Grain of Sand"

But this was short-lived. In a different mood in August 1969, he withdrew the offer to work on "scrambled pages, mostly bullshit." He'd "never had the vaguest idea what the book was supposed to be about."

I've changed the working title about 15 times—which is a fair indicator of my focus. At times it looks like a series of articles, but sometimes it looks like a novel with a few article fragments thrown in for fillers. I have no idea what Jim expects, or what he thinks I'm working on. All he ever said about it was "go write about the American Dream." Which is like saying "go write about the world..." The H. A. book was about the American Dream.

Anyway I don't want to burden you with all this. My point is that you shouldn't stack your work-schedule around anything connected to this pile of doomed bullshit I'm fighting with. . . .

And so much for that. I suspect you should go ahead with any other jobs you have in mind, because there's no sense talking about this for a while . . . a stupid, useless tangle of commercial arguments, bad contracts, surface compromises and well....to hell with it. I guess Jim will contact you if he ever gets a ms. to work on. OK for now....HST

What is your N. C. address?

To Jim Silberman he bemoaned the lack of perspective—that *single grain of sand* that if closely examined revealed a world. That is, "The job of a writer, it seems to me, is to focus very finely on a thing, a place, a person, act, phenomenon . . . and then, when the focus is right, to *understand,* and then *render* the subject of that focus in such a way that it suddenly appears in context—the reader's context, regardless of who the reader happens to be, or where." More precisely, "you focus on some scurvy freak in Oakland who calls himself a 'Hell's Angel' & write about him in such a way that any dingbat stockbroker in Cleveland can *see himself* somehow in the image of that scurvy freak."[63]

Instead of adjusting angles on a fine microscope, he was wrestling with an amorphous blob. Articles splattered. The *Esquire* NRA piece became bulky, ran to two hundred fifty pages. He tried to link Nixon, Chicago, the NRA. "The Death of the American Dream" hadn't whittled itself down to a topic that would provide him that fistful of concentration.

Roads change without a notice. I wonder what that road would have led down, and would I have taken it if the offer held up? Was I so dead set on Algeria there was no possibility of influence? I envisage now a hockey rink. The question is, *What team (future) is going to hit the puck into the safety net?* I answered this letter, but got no response until December.

Meanwhile, in a couple of not-overlooked remarks, Jan half indicated he wanted to marry me. For this was still not a torrid, blazing physical love affair. It was a deeply romantic question mark, a budding flower trying to develop full grown out of the five-year friendship. From Al Attafs "9/10" (October 9):

> You are my princess and I wish you were my queen. I'm sure with you I could stand all the many disenchantments that were waiting for me here. You've no idea of what the place I'm in can look like. It's a small town along the Algiers–Oran road, imagine some old Far-West place where

the houses would be in brick and the cow-boys wearing djellabas. . . . There's a tiny bar, primitive and crowded, where you enter through the back door and have your beer in a rush and with a shame-covered face. . . . The surroundings are desolate. A mud-carrying river, bare hills and the mountains in the distance. Everything reminding me of Mongolian Asia.

Still, I'm not sure so far I regret to have come. Having had plenty of time to think things over I've realised how important it is for me to get my degree. Days of wine and women, mirth and laughter, sermons and soda-water the day after have gone. If I were reasonable I'd fly back to Belgium, study, get my degree and, after having come to New York and asked you to marry me (will you?), go to some Embassy and live happily ever after. And I've got an idea that's what I'm going to do.

Write to me the very day you get this. I love you.

By October 31, Jean-Marie retracted his impulsive proposal:

If I was in a tiny town in Algeria I'm in a tiny hotel-room in Germany. . . . The idea behind this is that, if I get my degree in September I will have to go through those Embassy exams and German is one of the things required. . . . That's the story. It's kind of complicated and I find it hard to think that not even two weeks ago I was drinking my three-cents coffee in a hot little café of the Cheliff Valley and have been in Freiburg for one week already—I spent that week finding a room—but behind the meanders of it all there's one noble and beautiful thing: REASON. I've become reasonable or at least, I'm being in a reasonable mood. Since I failed in conquering my kingdom I want, at least, to be an Ambassador. If the mood lasts long enough, I will. A funny sort of, but still. . . . The day I'd fly to New

York you'd be the looser [*sic*] if you'd accepted me. It's an
eventuality that makes me doubt I'll ever come. But then I
still may come as a tourist, leaving ring and nosegay in the
cupboard where many another dream is withering (there's
a bit of Keats in this—do you think he's minding me?). If
I thought curiosity were one of your faults I might think I
didn't mention the three other ones so as to get an immediate answer.

However, the next letter was too ultradramatic to ignore.
Emotionally speaking, I was pulled back and forth: *Come. Don't.
Come to Algeria. No, I'm in Germany.* Not to mention the *on again, off
again* job offers from Hunter. I cannot remember all I was weighing
as players came and went.
At this point, Jean-Marie had clearly worked into the foreground.
He inspired me to breathlessness, a sense of urgency. The ultradra-
matic letter below came in November. He'd been called back from
Algeria when his grandmother died. Hoping to redirect him into a
diplomatic career, his family made the telegram sound as if it were his
mother. By the end of '69 he was at the Albert Ludwig University in
Freiburg, studying German to further that plan.
He again canceled out the invitation in the Algeria letter, but this
time sent up large red flags of imminent deadly danger:

> August (since, according to the date
> on your last letter, Greenville must still
> be living in that blessed month) 28

Dear Margaret,

Notice how the blue of my print has faded. It's all those
113 plus more pages of my novel. I hope, by this time, the
wandering letter will have arrived. I'm not going to repeat
what I said in it because I forgot ages ago what that was. I

have some vague notions. I think it was about Mensaert jr.
becoming serious and building up a new and totally different life where there would be no room for mirth and laughter and such follies as no serious-minded, forward-looking,
future-building man would accept or even consider without
a harsh laugh of contempt. The very contrary from what
I wrote on that postcard. I'm a torn man just now. I have
been living wild indeed, enjoyed it a lot, knew inwardly I'll
never be able to live otherwise, spend whole days and nights
in extreme-left stuben, improved my German a lot in, possibly, a one-sided way, played at a new game which takes two
men and two knives . . .

*Included was, again, a detail about his thought of suicide; in his last
moments it would have been "of you I think":*

Unfortunately, all these good things don't go without
a lot of drinking. Not that I have moral scruples against
drinking. On the contrary, I'm very indulgent as far as that
one of life's necessities is concerned. But somehow it doesn't
seem right for the soundness of my views on life and its
beauties manifold. My suicidal tendencies have come back.
They regularly appear after a certain amount of drinking.

That was it. I hurled myself into a rescue. I was hell-bent to waste
not a minute. Fly in. Once my emotions began to read the real feeling
underneath his dramatization, I was hooked. I believed in what was
possible. I saw it under imminent threat. I could stop it. Perhaps only
I could. I determined to jump again into a plane. Unsuspecting of
what I was really walking into seemingly with open eyes, but so much
hidden behind the shutters of what I didn't know—didn't know at
all. Jean-Marie would probably not have objected if I'd called the development "Here Comes Little Red Riding Hood," at least the facet
I downplayed if not in some ways ignored.

Perhaps if I'd had a better inner traffic cop . . .

It was not the most romantic wooing, to be told that in the very last moment of life it's "of you I think." But clearly a part of him, the real artist, did not want suicide; that part thrived in nondeveloped countries. That one could survive. And between the lines I read a true love poem.

I told my mother I was going to Germany. Would she drive me to the Raleigh–Durham Airport, not to mention pay for the ticket? And not even stop to swing by my father's office! Reluctantly she complied. That evening, my father, with whom I was so close, asked her if I were downstairs writing in the basement. She said no, on a plane to Germany!

To tell the truth, I guess I was in love with three people at the same time, in different parts of myself, in different ways. How could that be? How could that be?

Dashing into the tram in Freiburg, with heavy snow that made a fairyland of the trees, I went to the gasthaus address. I stood down on the ground floor. He was up on the stairs in a sort of suspended moment, in which he said, peering through the dim light, "Could you be Margaret?"

Gunnar, his best friend, was an impressive doctoral candidate in philosophy with a dissertation on Heraclitus. We went to bars, ate goulash, drank beer. Jan became fluent in German. Here, unlike in Morocco, was a real alcoholic. He often vomited when waking. That did not deter me. I thought if he were writing, his troubles would fade.

Proposing marriage several nights, he retracted the proposal the next day. And tested me in a horrible way, writing a letter about his awful traits—that he was a drunken, suicidal, pot smoking, irresponsible artist that no parents want their daughter near, or something to that effect—which he threatened to mail to my parents. Not that it wasn't true, but he put himself in the most shocking light. He didn't mail it, only threatened, dramatically, histrionically, lightly, engagingly, matter of factly. He warned me I should not marry him because

"You won't be able to accept I'll never do anything, be anybody. You won't be able to live a life with no tomorrow." He hesitated: "With a tomorrow, yes . . . but no day after tomorrow." Nothing swayed or deterred me. I was sure we were to marry.

I received a letter from Hunter written Dec. 13, '69—forwarded to Germany:

Dear M. A.,

Ho-ho, and late again. Not much to say either, except in terms of madness & bad scheduling on all fronts. I seem to have let everything drift for too long. Recently I spent 10 days in LA,* running totally amok in every way, crazed on rum and mescaline. Before that it was a savage election here. I ran a campaign that amounted to a takeover bid, and we lost by six votes.

Now I'm back here at this rotten machine, trying to hash together enough bullshit to satisfy Silberman and get that contract off my back. He no longer answers my letters. I'm convinced they think I've gone mad. Which may be true—although it only seems to come out when I sit down to write this thing I have no use for. On other fronts, I still function like a human being. But running out of money tends to narrow a man's vision somewhat, and that's my gig for now. Stone broke and flapping around like a jangled beast.

Are you off to Algeria yet? Where will this gibberish find you? Your talk (in an old letter) of pine trees and crickets got hold of me in a weird way. I keep remembering that line I quoted somewhere, by somebody—

---

*With his wife, trying to get her over a painful miscarriage, a baby they'd both wanted. This trauma, one can put into the chronology now. But at the time, he swallowed his grief and kept it to himself quite rightly. Also recovering from the hyper-intense Aspen mayor campaign.

"All my life my heart has sought a thing I cannot name."
Maybe it never existed. To be homesick for a myth is a form
of madness, I guess. So maybe they're right. All I know, for
now, is that I have to put a string of words together, in order
to pay my bills. But I can't get too excited about it. Neither
the writing nor the bills. What I'd really like to do right
now is spend about two weeks alone on a golf course, with
nobody else in sight...armed with a putter and two irons,
maybe a 3 and a 7...why not?

Anyway, I'm tired of this goddam
locked-in winter. Tired of the death and craziness in this
landscape. All of it. Everywhere I go people are cracking and
breaking and crumbling. Backing off and hunkering down.
My only real hope is that things are really as bad as they say.
That should give us some action. The more I think about
your "second life" notion, the more I think maybe you're
onto something. Let me know how it's working out.

                                                        Ciao, H

—Merry Christmas

Epilogue: How It's Working Out

I could not have predicted in my wildest dreams what the next chapter of my life would be like. The present memoir, in two volumes, was originally a single book. Some events in the first don't make sense till the second. I had listened carefully when Milton said, "Write it, your life, as you would write a novel" and would in the future when he commanded, "Don't let time measure *you*. *You* measure it." One thing I did not know was how neither Milton nor Jan would have been possible in my life without the other. They were essential bookends of my dreams and emotions: checks and balances of each other.

As the first volume ended and I found myself in Germany, I got a room on the floor below Jan. I was very happy and confident. I hadn't the least thought that he could settle into a conventional lifestyle. But I felt he would easily return to his carefree, productively artistic self once back in Morocco. What would it be like for me there? I should have been more skeptical, but I wasn't. Both of us, I imagined, would sit at our writing desks and be inspired.

There were warning signs already in Freiburg. I couldn't pull myself away from him long enough even to mail a letter at the post office. I was head first into a deep codependent relationship. And to top that, Jan was good at manipulating and blackmailing. I must keep emphasizing, though, that this was offset by high degrees of charm and imagination, and just plain fun and soaring thoughts.

I firmly believe that the surprising next chapters of my life would have been entirely different had I not had my writing, observing self trying to make sense of them, while my everyday self was vitally interested in what was going on.

Ours was not a cautious generation. Art is not cautious. To me, without a doubt life is purposeful and the meaning involves layers of truth, to quote Hunter. The adventurous years in volume two end up at the C. G. Jung Institute Zurich in 1986, brought there by the passing of Milton, who had continuously in a sense voiced my truth. Hunter will be in and out of the picture till our final meeting in person at Owl Farm. Yesterday I heard someone say—not to anyone in particular—in a group I was leading: "You have to do something that makes no sense, to reach something that makes total sense."

Notes

1. Faulkner, *Collected Stories*, 895.
2. Plimpton, *Shadow Box*, 337.
3. Koestler, "The Pioneer Beyond the Pale," 23.
4. *New York Herald Tribune*, May 31, 1963.
5. http://www.time.com/time/magazine/article /0,9171,896888,00.html
6. Written and sung by Gale Garnett, 1964.
7. Cowley, *A Second Flowering*, 57.
8. Harrell, *A Lecture Upon the Shadow*. In manuscript.
9. Redmond, "A Trip to Greece and Cyprus."
10. Thomas, "The Most Dangerous Man in Publishing,"1.
11. Krim, "Two Teachers—Nuts, Two Human Beings!" in *Views of a Nearsighted Cannoneer*, 229.
12. Klonsky, "A Writer's Education," in *A Discourse on Hip*, 42.
13. Krim, *Nearsighted Cannoneer*, 229–231.
14. Ibid., 230.
15. Diamond, "The Resurrection of Seymour Krim."
16. Elman, *Namedropping*, 75.
17. Krim, *Nearsighted Cannoneer*, 253.
18. "Cyril Connolly Quotes—The Quotations Page."
19. Harrell, "From Egypt to the Present," in Museum het Toreke's e-book Life, Page One, 9.
20. Vetter, "Hunter Thompson: A Freewheeling Conversation with the Outlaw Journalist and Only Man Alive to Ride with Both Richard Nixon and the Hell's Angels."
21. Thompson, *The Proud Highway. The Fear and Loathing Letters* 1: 429, 524.
22. Ibid., 541.
23. Ibid., 529.
24. Ibid., 569, 573.

25. Thompson, *Hell's Angels*, 24.
26. Ibid., 29.
27. Ibid., 27
28. Ibid., 274–275; 259–260.
29. Ibid., 128.
30. Sentinel, "Eugene W. McGarr Is Dead."
31. The "pleasantest visual memory" comment comes from a Bill Kennedy email to me May 16, 2010. The rest, from a telephone conversation in 2009.
32. Davis, "Interview with Host Alan Davis and Hell's Angel Cliff 'Skip' Workman," in *Ancient Gonzo Wisdom*, 6; Bulger, "The Hunter S. Thompson Interview"; *Fear and Loathing Letters* 1, 609.
33. Steadman, The Joke's Over, 271.
34. Vetter, "Freewheeling Conversation."
35. Ibid.
36. Thompson, *Songs of the Doomed*, 114.
37. Thompson, *Fear and Loathing Letters* 1: 608.
38. Thompson, *The Great Shark Hunt*, 83.
39. Thompson, *Fear and Loathing Letters* 1: 618.
40. Thorpe, "Books: A Masterpiece on Waning of Censorship."
41. Thompson, *Fear and Loathing Letters* 1: 645–647.
42. "First NYC Major Revival of 'The Beard' by Michael McClure," *New York Theater Wire*.
43. Perry, 117–118.
44. Thompson, *Fear and Loathing in America*. Gonzo Letters 2:14.
45. Thompson: *Fear and Loathing: On the Campaign Trail*, 232–233.
46. Perry, 120.
47. Markowitz, "Bedtime for Gonzo: Grappling with the Legend of Hunter S. Thompson."
48. Thompson, *The Great Shark Hunt*, 126–127.
49. Thompson, *Gonzo Letters* 2: 35–36.

50. This letter and Hunter's answer are reprinted in *Gonzo Letters* 2: 72–73, 85, along with the letter he sent to me and the enclosed letter to Carol Hoffman, 89–90.
51. *Time*, "Nation: Daley City under Siege," August 30, '68.
52. Thompson, *Kingdom of Fear*, 79–82.
53. Thompson, *Gonzo Letters* 2: 119.
54. Ibid., 118.
55. Ibid., 146.
56. Thompson, *Campaign Trail*, 10.
57. Thompson, "Memoirs of a Wretched Weekend in Washington," 178–179.
58. Thompson, *Gonzo Letters* 2: 158.
59. Thompson, *The Great Shark Hunt*, 168.
60. Thompson, *Gonzo Letters* 2: 178ff.
61. Thompson, *The Great Shark Hunt*, 94–95.
62. Thompson, *Gonzo Letters* 2, 270, 269.
63. Ibid., 205, 264.

Works Cited

HUNTER S. THOMPSON BOOKS IN ORDER OF PUBLICATION

Hell's Angels: The Strange and Terrible Saga of the Outlaw Motorcycle Gangs. New York: Random House, 1967.

Fear and Loathing in Las Vegas: A Savage Journey to the Heart of the American Dream. New York: Random House, 1971. First published in *Rolling Stone* issue 95, November 11, 1971, and issue 96, November 25, 1971.

Fear and Loathing: On the Campaign Trail '72. 1973. Reprint, New York: Warner Books, 2006.

The Great Shark Hunt: Strange Tales from a Strange Time. Gonzo Papers vol. 1. 1979. Reprint, New York: Simon & Schuster, 2003.

Songs of the Doomed: More Notes on the Death of the American Dream. Gonzo Papers vol. 3. New York: Summit Books, 1990.

The Proud Highway: Saga of a Desperate Southern Gentleman, 1955–1967. The Fear and Loathing Letters vol. 1. Edited by Douglas Brinkley. London: Bloomsbury Publishing Plc., 1997.

Fear and Loathing in America: The Brutal Odyssey of an Outlaw Journalist, 1968–1976. The Gonzo Letters vol. 2. Edited by Douglas Brinkley. New York: Simon & Schuster, 2000.

Kingdom of Fear: Loathsome Secrets of a Star-Crossed Child in the Final Days of the American Century. New York: Simon & Schuster, 2003.

Booklet: The Gonzo Tapes: The Life and Work of Dr. Hunter S. Thompson. Prepared by Alex Gibney and collaborators. Los Angeles: The Shout Factory, 2008.

HUNTER S. THOMPSON ARTICLES IN ORDER OF PUBLICATION

"Memoirs of a Wretched Weekend in Washington." *Boston Globe,* February 23, 1969. Reprint. In *The Great Shark Hunt,* 177–182.

"The Temptations of Jean-Claude Killy." *Scanlan's Monthly,* March 1970. Reprint. In *The Great Shark Hunt,* 77–96.

"The Kentucky Derby Is Decadent and Depraved." *Scanlan's Monthly,* June 1970. Reprint. In *Fear and Loathing in Las Vegas and Other American Stories,* 263–283. New York: Random House Modern Library, 1996.

"Strange Rumblings in Aztlan." *Rolling Stone,* April 29, 1971. Reprint. In *The Great Shark Hunt,* 119–151.

HUNTER S. THOMPSON INTERVIEWS IN ORDER OF APPEARANCE

Davis, Alan. "Interview with Host Alan Davis and Hell's Angel Cliff 'Skip' Workman," *Sunday,* Canadian Broadcasting Corporation, March 1967. Reprint. In *Ancient Gonzo Wisdom: Interviews with Hunter S. Thompson,* 5–8. Edited by Anita Thompson. Cambridge, MA: Da Capo Press, 2009.

Vetter, Craig. "Hunter Thompson: A Freewheeling Conversation with the Outlaw Journalist and Only Man Alive to Ride with Both Richard Nixon and the Hell's Angels," *Playboy.* November 1974. http://www.playboy.com/articles/hunter-s-thompson-interview/index. html?page=1; http://www.playboy.com/articles/hunter-s-thompson-interview/index. html?page=2.

Bulger, Adam. "The Hunter S. Thompson Interview," *Freezerbox Magazine.* March 9, 2004. http://www.freezerbox.com/archive/article.php?id=287.

BIBLIOGRAPHY OF OTHER AUTHORS

Anonymous. *Madame Solario.* New York: Viking Press, 1956.

Brinkley, Douglas. Editor's Note to *Fear and Loathing in America,* xiv–xxii.

Connolly, Cyril. "Cyril Connolly Quotes—The Quotations Page." http://www.quotationspage.com/quotes/Cyril_Connolly/.

Cowley, Malcolm. *A Second Flowering: Works and Days of the Lost Generation.* 1973. Reprint. New York: Penguin Books, 1980.

Diamond, Jason. "The Resurrection of Seymour Krim," Arts & Culture, *Jewcy*, June 28, 2010. http://www.jewcy.com/arts-and-culture/ resurrection_seymour_krim.

Elman, Richard M. *Namedropping: Mostly Literary Memoirs.* New York: State University of New York Press, 1999.

Faulkner, William. "Carcassonne." In *Collected Stories of William Faulkner,* 895–900. New York: Vintage, 1995.

"First NYC Major Revival of 'The Beard' by Michael McClure," *New York Theatre Wire.* http://www.nytheatre-wire.com/beard.htm.

Flynn, Marty. "Scanlan's Issue 1: Hunter S. Thompson, Jean-Claude Killy." Hunter S. Thompson Books, http://hstbooks. org/2008/07/08/scanlans-issue-1-hunter-s-thompson-jean-claude-killy/

Harrell, Margaret A. *A Lecture Upon the Shadow.* In manuscript.

——. "From Egypt to the Present." In Jan Mensaert et al. *Life, Page One.* Edited by Margaret A. Harrell. Tienen, Belgium: Museum het Toreke, 2001. Part of *The Life & Works of Jan Mensaert* (exhibit), coordinated by the museum director, Staf Thomas.

——. *Love in Transition: Voyage of Ulysses—Letters to Penelope.* Vol. 1–2. Sibiu, Romania: Hermann Press, 1996.

Klonsky, Milton. "A Writer's Education." 1982. Reprint. In *A Discourse on Hip: Selected Writings of Milton Klonsky,* 42–46. Edited by Ted Solotaroff. Detroit: Wayne State Univ. Press, 1991. First published in *New York Times Book Review,* March 7, 1982, as part of Milton Klonsky's obituary.

Koestler, Arthur. "The Pioneer Beyond the Pale," *Observer* (London), May 7, 1961, 23–24.

Krassner, Paul. "Blowing Deadlines with Hunter Thompson." In *One Hand Jerking: Reports From an Investigative Satirist.* Reprint. Email from Krassner to me December 27, '06.

Krim, Seymour. "From *Two Teachers—Nuts, Two Human Beings!*" 1961. Reprint. In *Views of a Nearsighted Cannoneer,* 226–256. Exp. ed. New York: E. P. Dutton & Co., 1968. Later reprinted as "Milton Klonsky" in *What's This Cat's Story? The Best of Seymour Krim.* St. Paul: MN. Paragon House, 1991. Also reprinted in Mark Cohen, ed., *Missing a Beat: The Rants and Regrets of Seymour Krim*, 2010.

Markowitz, Andy. "Bedtime for Gonzo: Grappling with the Legend of Hunter S. Thompson," The Arts: Book Reviews, *City Paper* (Baltimore), March 28, 2001. http://www.citypaper.com/arts/review.asp?rid=5133.

McClure, Michael. *The Beard.* Limited ed. San Francisco: Coyote Books, March 1967.

McKeen, William. *Outlaw Journalist: The Life and Times of Hunter S. Thompson.* New York: W. W. Norton & Co., 2008.

"Nation: Daley City under Siege," *Time*, August 30, '68. http://www.time.com/time/magazine/article/0,9171,844571,00.html.

Nichols, John. "Hunter Thompson's Political Genius," *The Nation*, February 22, '05. http://www.thenation.com/blog/hunter-thompsons-political-genius.

Perry, Paul. *Fear and Loathing: The Strange and Terrible Saga of Hunter S. Thompson.* New York: Thunder's Mouth Press, 1992.

Plimpton, George. *Shadow Box: An Amateur in the Ring.* Guilford, CT: The Globe Pequot Press/The Lyons Press, 2003.

Redmond, Layne. "A Trip to Greece and Cyprus," May 2005. http://randyroark.com/a-trip-to-greece-and-cyprus-an-exploration-of-sacredness-oracles-and-the-power-of-drumming-with-layne-redmond-may-2005/

Sentinel. "Eugene W. McGarr Is Dead." *Rants N Raves,* June 26, 2007. http://www.rantsnraves.org/showthread.php?557-Eugene-W.-McGarr-is-Dead.

Steadman, Ralph. *The Joke's Over: Bruised Memories: Gonzo, Hunter S. Thompson, and Me.* Boston: Houghton Mifflin Harcourt, 2006.

Thomas, Louisa. "The Most Dangerous Man in Publishing," *Newsweek*, December 6, 2008, 1–7. http://www.newsweek.com/id/172555.

Thorpe, Day. "Books: A Masterpiece on Waning of Censorship," *Washington Star*, n.d.

Wenner, Jann S., and Corey Seymour. *Gonzo: The Life of Hunter S. Thompson*. New York: Little, Brown & Co., 2007.

Index

Look for Volume II

The author of eight books in the *Love in Transition: Voyage of Ulysses—Letters to Penelope* nonfiction series, including *Toward a Philosophy of Perception*, Harrell copy edited Hunter S. Thompson's first book, *Hell's Angels*, at Random House. HST acknowledged her in *Gonzo Letters* 2. Between 1996 and 2001 she was international editing coordinator for a "het Toreke" (Belgium) museum exhibit on Jan Mensaert. Since 1995 she has been in the Marquis *Who's Who in the World* and similar publications, including *Who's Who in American Art* for cloud photography, which she exhibited in Romania, Canada, etc. Since returning to the United States in 2001 she has taught personal-growth guided-meditation courses through "the light body." Academically, she earned a BA from Duke University (Honors and Distinction in History) and an MA from Columbia University (literature) and studied postgraduate at the C. G. Jung Institute, Zurich. To learn more, visit her at http://www.hunterthompsonnewbook. com, http://www.cloudgiclee.com, and http://www.lightangel.net.

CPSIA information can be obtained at www.ICGtesting.com
Printed in the USA
BVOW011104140512

290161BV00011B/246/P